Getting to Grips with Doctoral Research

CW00553206

Palgrave Study Skills

Business Degree Success
Career Skills
Cite Them Right (8th edn)
Critical Thinking Skills (2nd edn)
e-Learning Skills (2nd edn)
The Exam Skills Handbook (2nd edn)
Great Ways to Learn Anatomy and Physiology
How to Begin Studying English Literature
   (3rd edn)
How to Manage Your Distance and Open
   Learning Course
How to Manage Your Postgraduate Course
How to Study Foreign Languages
How to Study Linguistics (2nd edn)
How to Use Your Reading in Your Essays
How to Write Better Essays (2nd edn)
How to Write Your Undergraduate Dissertation
Information Skills
The International Student Handbook
IT Skills for Successful Study
The Mature Student's Guide to Writing
   (3rd edn)
The Mature Student's Handbook
The Palgrave Student Planner
Practical Criticism
Presentation Skills for Students (2nd edn)

The Principles of Writing in Psychology
Professional writing (2nd edn)
Researching Online
Skills for Success (2nd edn)
The Student's Guide to Writing (3rd edn)
Study Skills Connected
Study Skills for International Postgraduates
The Study Skills Handbook (3rd edn)
Study Skills for Speakers of English as a
   Second Language
Studying History (3rd edn)
Studying Law (3rd edn)
Studying Modern Drama (2nd edn)
Studying Psychology (2nd edn)
Teaching Study Skills and Supporting Learning
The Undergraduate Research Handbook
The Work-Based Learning Student Handbook
Work Placements – A Survival Guide for
   Students
Write it Right (2nd edn)
Writing for Engineers (3rd edn)
Writing for Law
Writing for Nursing and Midwifery Students
   (2nd edn)
You2Uni

Pocket Study Skills

14 Days to Exam Success
Blogs, Wikis, Podcasts and More
Brilliant Writing Tips for Students
Completing Your PhD
Doing Research
Getting Critical
Planning Your Essay
Planning Your PhD
Reading and Making Notes

Referencing and Understanding Plagiarism
Reflective Writing
Report Writing
Science Study Skills
Studying with Dyslexia
Success in Groupwork
Time Management
Writing for University

Palgrave Research Skills

Authoring a PhD
The Foundations of Research (2nd edn)
Getting to Grips with Doctoral Research
The Good Supervisor (2nd edn)

The Postgraduate Research Handbook
   (2nd edn)
Structuring Your Research Thesis

For a complete listing of all our titles in this area please visit www.palgrave.com/studyskills

Getting to Grips with Doctoral Research

Margaret Walshaw

First published 2012 by
PALGRAVE MACMILLAN

Palgrave Macmillan in the UK is an imprint of Macmillan Publishers Limited,
registered in England, company number 785998, of Houndmills, Basingstoke,
Hampshire RG21 6XS.

Palgrave Macmillan in the US is a division of St Martin's Press LLC,
175 Fifth Avenue, New York, NY 10010.

Palgrave Macmillan is the global academic imprint of the above companies
and has companies and representatives throughout the world.

Palgrave® and Macmillan® are registered trademarks in the United States,
the United Kingdom, Europe and other countries

ISBN: 978-0-230-36955-9

This book is printed on paper suitable for recycling and made from fully
managed and sustained forest sources. Logging, pulping and manufacturing
processes are expected to conform to the environmental regulations of the
country of origin.

A catalogue record for this book is available from the British Library.

A catalog record for this book is available from the Library of Congress.

10 9 8 7 6 5 4 3 2 1
21 20 19 18 17 16 15 14 13 12

Printed and bound in Great Britain by
CPI Antony Rowe, Chippenham and Eastbourne

Contents

Introduction: Getting Introduced to Doctoral Study

This book is a guide to your doctoral study in social science. It will provide you with assistance to help you successfully complete your study in a timely fashion. If you are considering enrolling in a doctoral programme at a tertiary institution sometime in the future, the book will help you prepare for the experience by demystifying the process and providing you with a better understanding of the doctoral process and the requirements for success. If you are already enrolled in a doctoral programme, you will also benefit from the advice offered in this book by developing a deeper understanding of the process that will allow you to enrich your doctoral experience.

Doctoral education is a key growth area for universities. More students than ever, and not solely lifetime career academics, are deciding to embark on doctoral study. Ranging in age from twenties to over eighty, they bring widely diverse backgrounds, needs, cultures, languages, religious affiliations and experiences to their study, all of which serve to influence their doctoral work. No longer considered as apprentices to a guild, today's doctoral students undertake study with a view towards advancing their careers. Increasingly, doctoral education is seen as a form of research training that requires not only project completion and a thesis, but also explicit attention to the development of transferable skills and competencies that will prepare the successful doctoral student for employment in diverse contexts. The quality of such education is measured by timely completions, levels of candidate satisfaction and attention to the effectiveness of supervision.

The traditional pathway is through a PhD programme of full-time study. This programme suits many local and international students who are able to devote their full attention and time to their study. Many doctoral programmes are now available part-time and this provides students with the flexibility to both study and continue to work in paid employment. Some programmes comprise a structured suite of high-level papers followed by a thesis investigation. Whatever programme of doctoral study you intend to enrol in or are already enrolled in, the same standards of discipline, rigour and scholarship apply, as do the same measures of success.

Statistics have shown that, irrespective of the doctoral programme enrolled in, many doctoral students do not complete their study. Difficulties associated with timely completion provide compelling reasons for a text like this, aimed specifically at you, the doctoral student. This book will scaffold you through the many aspects of the doctoral journey, explaining the processes and milestones involved in doctoral study. It will offer assistance with the mechanics of doing a doctorate, by clarifying expectations and conventions of doctoral study and writing. It will enable you to see more clearly what you want to research, how to go about it and how to work towards achieving your aim to produce a good quality thesis. As well as learning about research techniques, you will develop the important skills of formulating research questions, synthesising the literature, and developing critical, logical and lateral thinking. You will learn what it means to conduct research in a safe, ethical and sensitive manner, and to confront the fundamental question of why your research might be worth doing and how to communicate what others might learn from it.

Achieving success in your doctoral study is not simply about enhancing your skills base to design an achievable project. It is a complex, original and creative activity that takes place in an institutional environment in which procedures are often not made transparent and in which criteria for success are often not clearly articulated. Achieving success is about learning how to maximise your learning opportunities through day-to-day processes and learning how to develop constructive personal interactions that will impact positively on your doctoral journey. Engagement in the doctoral programme is shaped by support and interrelationships with a number of significant others, not the least being your supervisory team. It is fair to say that institutional practices and values, supervision and peer cultures help shape your experiences in no small way. All will have significant effects on your behavioural, emotional and cognitive engagement with your doctoral study.

The privilege of doctoral study brings its own responsibilities. By taking control of and responsibility for your studies, you will be able to navigate your way successfully through institutional processes and working relationships with others. You will learn how to avoid needless mistakes and be on the alert for risks and dangers that can be costly in terms of time, research quality and finance. Of course, this book cannot guarantee absolute success, but what it can do is help develop your knowledge, skills and capabilities. Importantly, it can deepen your understanding not only of your work but also of yourself. It will point to where to go next in order to build on your progress, and highlight what needs to be done to stay focused, to keep control, and to keep the momentum going over time. Ultimately, your proactive involvement in your study will lead to a positive doctoral experience and successful, timely completion.

The book draws on solid research-based evidence. Backdropped by international research in the field, it is also closely informed by my empirical research undertaken with doctoral students. From data generated from surveys and individual interviews, it has become clear that doctoral education is poorly understood by many students involved in doctoral study. What is apparent is that students want to widen their understanding of what it means to conduct research at the doctoral level. They also want to learn how to deal with the isolation and confusion as well as the dilemmas and difficulties that are typically encountered during the doctoral journey. My experiences as a doctoral supervisor and a doctorate programme coordinator within my university also bring useful points to the discussion, as well as starters for sound advice and opportunities for your personal and academic growth.

You will be well prepared to meet the challenges and demands of your doctoral study head on.

● Overview of chapters

The book consists of nine chapters:

1. Getting started
2. Getting a handle on the topic, questions and the literature
3. Getting close to theory
4. Getting designs on methods
5. Getting underway with the research proposal
6. Getting alongside support
7. Getting on with writing
8. Getting examined
9. Getting your research 'out there'

Chapter 1 gets to grips with what doctoral study is about. It sets the scene by providing an information base for your future work. It is intended to correct any misunderstandings you have about what doctoral study involves and to minimise any doubts about your own chances of success. The point made is that research is fundamental to doctoral study and is the medium through which you will be able to address social science questions that are of specific interest to you. The chapter provides a starting place for understanding the research process. It outlines what it means to be a researcher and what you need to know to begin conducting research.

One of the sheer joys in participating in a doctoral programme is in seeing how your personal learning escalates. Of course, such learning brings new challenges and demands and the chapter asks you to confront your current situation and your reasons for your intention to study for a doctorate. It emphasises what is important for succeeding in doctoral study and the study habits and skills base you will need in order to undertake what might turn out to be the biggest and most intensive piece of work that you will ever do. Modes of working bring particular advantages as well as disadvantages to your study and this chapter makes suggestions for succeeding, whether you are studying on or off campus. The chapter ends with a look ahead at the doctoral process.

Chapter 2 allows you to get a handle on the topic, questions and the literature. It focuses on the decisions you must make, and gives guidance in refining a research topic and making it researchable and manageable through the questions you ask. Getting a handle on the general topic area is quite straightforward but turning a topic area into something researchable is not so easy. This chapter guides you into formulating a research problem that is clearly and closely defined, is significant, is grounded in the literature and, above all, is able to be researched. Following on from the research problem, you receive guidance into developing a research question. The point emphasised is that the development of a good research question is one of the most important skills that a researcher needs.

It is important to read widely. Reading and thinking about as well as evaluating the literature on your topic are critical stages in the planning of your research. This chapter helps you develop the specific skills and knowledge that will allow you to analyse and synthesise the literature in a way that resembles an essay with an important message rather than a series of disconnected commentaries. It will help you to identify gaps in the research, and to justify and build a case for conducting your own study. The requirements of referencing are explained.

Chapter 3 explores social science as a field underpinned by a range of theoretical approaches. While assumptions about what counts as quality in research are sometimes shared amongst groups of researchers, different understandings about the nature of knowledge and truth, values, and being all significantly influence the way in which research is framed. The chapter provides an arresting reminder that the researcher's world view figures significantly in all the decisions made in relation to the research, and draws attention to the implications of researching in contexts in which other world views are prevalent.

Each theory has its own coherent set of ideas, values and assumptions, and each has something important to tell us about the shape and character of society. Each leads to different views about how the research might be undertaken. The topic chosen, the questions asked, the research methods employed, the analysis and the discussion of the findings, even the writing itself, are all directly associated with the researcher's theoretical stance. Tracing a number of major theories in social science allows you to consider the possibilities and to determine with which theoretical position you might best guide your research. It provides you with an opportunity to think through the implications of following a line of inquiry from a specific theoretical position.

Chapter 4 helps you get designs on research methods. Because social science issues involve social relations and processes, they are typically multifaceted. Rather than offering universal checklists for undertaking research, what this chapter does is emphasise that there are often multiple ways of carrying out research. This means that there is no consensus about the kind of methodology that research will take. In a field where there is no canon and where there are no core methods, research cannot be undertaken with a prescribed recipe approach.

In this chapter we look at a range of methods and strategies used in social science research. While most research is empirical research, it is not uncommon for doctoral students to undertake theoretical research, analytical research or conceptual-philosophical research. Each requires different kinds of methodological tools. We explore the more common research methodologies and look at what is involved with surveys, interviewing and observation. We note the place of pilot studies and emphasise the importance of addressing ethical issues in relation to the conduct of the research.

Chapter 5 takes you through the development of a research proposal. A research proposal is a central feature of the research world and the first step researchers take before they conduct their research. All researchers, including doctoral students, must write a plan to clarify to others (and to themselves) what topic is going to be investigated and why it is important, what processes and procedures will be used, and what they expect to find out from the research. Whilst there is generally no set format for the proposal, there are, however, key sections and headings that will allow you to put a strong case forward for your study. This chapter guides you towards a suitable proposal structure.

One thing that new researchers quickly learn from writing a research proposal is that the proposal itself is a form of research. Explaining and justifying your proposed study to readers requires a clear conceptual framework to put forward a case or argument for your study. It requires thinking, searching, sourcing material, and making firm decisions about a range of aspects that will contribute to your study – aspects such as what literature to include, what research design to use, and who will participate in the study.

Chapter 6 explores the structured support of supervisors that is available to you during the doctoral process. Doctoral study can be a lonely experience. For one thing, it is a lengthy process; for another, it demands independence. Ultimately the responsibility of succeeding is yours. However, if you take advantage of the assistance on offer from a range of sources then problems will be minimised and your study will turn into an enriching experience.

Supervisors are the primary means of support during the doctoral journey. They are experienced researchers with a wealth of expertise that will provide you with the knowledge to scaffold your study and to help you understand and engage with the culture of research. The chapter looks at the roles and responsibilities of both student and supervisor in the supervision relationship. It explores the varying ways that make the supervision relationship productive and effective. It emphasises the importance of developing shared understandings amongst those involved in the supervision in relation to the terms of the working relationship. The chapter also provides a discussion of the tensions that may arise within the supervision arrangement and provides guidance on ways to resolve issues and conflicts.

Chapter 7 provides guidance about writing the doctoral thesis. While there are no hard and fast rules about the writing in a thesis, you will notice that a great deal of similarity in presentation style and structure exists between theses. In this chapter you will learn about common approaches, sections and headings. This chapter assists you in developing a skill set that includes a demonstration of your competence in writing a comprehensive literature review; in making sense of and handling the data; in explaining, summarising and explaining your results in relation to the existing literature; in drawing conclusions that are relevant to the research community; and in complying with conventions for referencing and quotations. These skills go some way to demonstrate that your thesis represents a scholarly, relevant and contemporary account of a study at a level appropriate to doctoral study.

However, skills and technical elegance are only part of the requirements. The thesis must present an explicit argument. It is particularly important to identify your standpoint and to make clear the contribution of your research to the wider research community, and to identify what advances in theory, concepts or methodology your thesis provides. The chapter highlights the importance of being clear and focused in telling the reader about the context and about what you actually did in your study; about who was involved; about clarifying your definitions; about explaining the theories that underpin the study; about providing evidence of critical evaluation, particularly of the literature; about offering explicit evidence for the claims you make; and about acknowledging the limitations and wider significance of your findings.

Chapter 8 takes you into the stage after you have submitted your thesis. The examination process that follows typically involves independent written assessments of your work from examiners and a viva (oral) examination or defence. Together, they represent the means by which you will be identified as a competent researcher. What the examiners will look for is your ability to undertake original research. They will also be looking for intellectual depth and rigour and a demonstration of your independence as a researcher. It will be important that your work demonstrates clear organisation, logical coherence and strong consistency.

The viva or defence complements and adds strength to the written reports of the examiners. It is not a mere formality. Talking about your work in a way that is convincing to experts in the field is quite different from writing about what you did and found and the significance of the findings. For that reason, the way you articulate your thoughts about the work and the way you present yourself at the viva or defence will play a critical role in the assessment of your work. The chapter explores ways in which you can successfully join the scholarly debate around your topic with your examiners.

Chapter 9 marks endings and new beginnings. The chapter moves you into the stage when the thesis examination is over and any emendations have been approved. It makes the important point that your work as a researcher is now officially recognised. In light of this, many doctoral candidates believe that a completed thesis is the end point of their work as a researcher. This chapter takes a different stance, proposing that your researcher-life is merely beginning. This is a thought-provoking proposal, and we expand on this by looking at the expectations placed on you once you have completed.

This final chapter in *Getting to Grips with Doctoral Research* explores the avenues for getting your research 'out there' into the research and wider communities. It pays attention to the requirements for writing for academic publications and to writing for professional journals. Of course this is not to imply that other approaches to dissemination are not useful. To the contrary, presentations to local communities, media reports, and other forms of dissemination of your work are all encouraged. What the chapter does suggest is that your findings have the potential to clear a space for new insight and for imagining creative change.

● A note on the use of this book

There are a number of ways you can use this text. The structure of the book is designed to help you come to terms with new knowledge and skills in a systematic way. The book offers suggestions about undertaking a doctorate. It is not a 'how to' manual that gives you rules and steps to follow. Instead, it is more of a guide that will equip you with the tools to think with dexterity as you make your way through various aspects of your doctoral work. It is designed to sharpen your thinking and hone your skills and crafts for bringing critical inquiry to bear on your research interest.

Readers either contemplating or newly enrolled in a doctorate programme will find the order of the chapters useful for developing new understandings about the doctoral experience. Readers further on in their doctoral study may prefer to be selective and may want to begin reading the chapters in the order that suits their current stage on the doctoral journey. Whatever order you read the book, it is there to be used iteratively, shaping and reshaping understanding, in response to your own continuing questions and pursuit of knowledge.

Each chapter begins with an overview of the key concepts or themes discussed in that chapter and ends with a summary of the main points and key terms covered. Most chapters include case study stories that provide an avenue for sharing experiences and bring the doctoral journey to life. Some data come from my own research on and experience in doctoral education. Some examples are fictitious and have been created to emphasise specific points. All of the research participants whose stories are used have given their permission for the use of the transcripts. Following my ethical obligations to these participants, I have given them fictitious names.

I hope that you will act upon the activities offered. They are there as opportunities to develop wider understandings and to manage your research by developing strategies and plans for the doctoral process. After working with the activities and the case studies, take some time to reflect on how those new understandings help you refine, sharpen or enrich your own work in relation to the chapter topic.

I wish you all the best for your doctoral studies. Eventually, I am confident, the award will be yours.

1 Getting Started

● What's different about a doctorate?

Beginning a doctorate is both an exciting and a daunting undertaking. It's exciting because it represents a period of intense personal growth and professional development. As well, it carries the potential for new career opportunities and the possibilities for entry into academia. However, beginning a doctorate is also daunting because this degree is a programme of high-level study and research and represents a major academic commitment. What you need to be aware of is that the anticipated hard work ahead is guaranteed to be compensated for by the sense of intense personal satisfaction in achieving the highest formal university qualification. Any personal doubts can be cast aside knowing that once you have completed you will have made your entrance within the social science community as a competent researcher.

Whichever programme of study you are enrolled in, the doctorate is considered as a training programme since its focus is towards producing skills development, competence and independence in researching, as well as professional recognition. You will be expected to produce a thesis that is bigger than anything you have ever written before. Quite likely, the mega-text will lie somewhere between 70,000 and 100,000 words. It will require you to carry out research through the full cycle of planning, action, drawing conclusions and communicating. What you need to be aware of is that it is the contribution to knowledge that will differentiate your doctoral study from any other study you have embarked on. In the past what you learned was knowledge that other people offered. That kind of learning is, of course, critically important. However, what is paramount in doctoral study is that you work at a level that will allow you to produce significant and original work. This is what will mark you out as a researcher. If you demonstrate that you can work at this level through your thesis then you will be awarded the title of 'doctor' as a public statement and recognition of your achievement. You will also be given the licence to carry out further research and, as well, to supervise other research students. More than that, others will read what you have to say. In time, they will develop your work to make a further difference to social science.

If this sounds exciting, then well and good. If it sounds like a formidable task, the advice is don't give up on doctoral study. It is true that doctoral study is a long-term and full-on commitment. However, keep in mind that if you meet the fairly stringent entry requirements for a doctoral programme of study, then a doctorate is definitely within your reach. But let's be realistic, things do not always go according to plan. Supervisors change universities, research participants become unavailable, interviews fail to record, your proposed theory doesn't seem to work, family dynamics change. These are the kinds of challenges that researchers face. In the lowest hours of your study remember that your university believes you will succeed. Others, too, believe in you. Be sure to count on them to keep you going and help you find a way to deal with difficulties.

> **"**At the beginning I had the feeling that doing a doctorate was really overwhelming. I felt the process was extremely challenging – certainly at the beginning – and I wondered at times whether or not I had the capabilities to manage it. Now coming out at the other end – which I almost am – I think that it's a huge source of pleasure. The satisfaction to see that, actually, I had managed it and I had managed it reasonably well, is probably the biggest pleasure.**"**

The fact that you are already searching for advice on doctoral study sends a clear message that you are taking charge of your learning, that you can work independently, that you can plan for success. These are attributes that are highly valued in doctoral study. On your doctoral journey you will learn new skills and develop new insights that, together, signal a major learning accomplishment. A defining moment for many doctoral students occurs, sometimes at the completion of the work, when the various aspects of the thesis are conceptualised together and made to make sense. The research problem, the questions, the literature that propels those questions, as well as the methodology, analysis and discussion, and the theory underpinning these, all play a part in the creation of new insights from the completion of a responsible and sound piece of research.

There is no curriculum for a doctorate and you are the one responsible for your progress. In that sense, then, the doctorate is a step up in personal learning that not everyone is privileged to experience. What sets it apart from earlier study is that it seeks explanations, extends understandings, tests predictions and operates at a level beyond the descriptive. It goes without saying that the step up brings new challenges and demands, both intellectually and emotionally, so the decision to embark on doctoral education is not to be taken lightly. You need to be sure that you really do want to do this work, that you know what the work entails, that you can commit to it, and that you will be motivated to continue. When you are convinced, make the most of the rare opportunity given to you to create new knowledge for yourself as well as for the research community. Your proactive engagement, enthusiasm and determination will help keep fears of failure at bay.

What's important to realise is that the step up in learning that goes hand in hand with doctoral study also brings rewards and high levels of creativity and productive work. Looking to the future to the time when you complete your doctorate, you will have learned so much about your particular topic of study, and, successful doctoral students tell us, you will learn so much about yourself from the experience. At this early stage of your study it is important to address the issue of your personal motivation for studying the advanced degree.

> *"I got to the point in my job where I felt that I needed a new challenge. And I just love the academic environment. I like the academic challenge and, you know, pushing myself. There was that feeling that I hadn't been stretched to my limit; I wanted to challenge myself further and see what I could do."*

> *"For me, doing a doctorate is pretty much pushed by my career. I'm a lecturer and it had been a requirement for a long time that I study for a doctorate. But after my Master's degree I had other responsibilities. I had a family to look after. Time passed by and ten years later I find myself involved in a PhD."*

> *"After finishing my Master's I was made redundant from my job and that caused me to have quite a serious rethink about what it was I wanted to do from that point forward. At that time I lived in a small community and it wasn't necessarily easy to find a similar sort of position to the one I had and that caused a lot of reflection. At that time I thought, well, if I was going to do a doctorate then this was probably a better time than any to start. I also had the feeling that if I didn't do it now I wouldn't do it. I didn't feel there would be an opportunity later on for me to come back to it."*

> *"Lots of personal reasons: I'd really enjoyed my Master's studies. I enjoyed the research and felt like I hadn't done as much as I wanted to in that topic. I wanted to continue. I had a feeling that, you know, I had just started and I'd like to do more."*

One student wants to uncover additional layers of an issue that he had explored in earlier research study. Another is confronted with changed circumstances that create an opportunity to study. One student wishes to

extend herself academically and one student is hoping to trade a doctoral
qualification for career promotion. These are all valid reasons for undertaking doctoral study. However, you might be surprised at how many students
enrol in a doctorate for the wrong reasons, and with dire consequences.
Many students do not understand the commitment required.

*"I have to use a lot of my own time and, you know, it's not unusual for me
to commit an entire weekend to working on my study. Usually I spend one
day in the weekend but if I have a milestone due it's both days."*

*"Sometimes I feel frustrated about how much time I'm having to spend
when I could be doing other things but I know that it's just a consequence of
being enrolled in a doctorate."*

*"I was working full-time and studying part-time and trying to balance them
both with home activities. Trying to balance the three wasn't always easy
and something had to give. Sometimes it was work, sometimes it was
home, and sometimes it was the PhD. But I recognised that there would be
personal gains for me so I expected to do it in personal time. And the odd
corner had to be cut here and there."*

Part-time students who continue with employment sometimes fail to set
aside sufficient time for the reading, data collection and analysis and, simply,
the clear thinking that is required in doctoral work. International students
and non-native English speakers sometimes fail to factor in the additional
time and effort required to get up to speed with the command of language
that is required. Completing the following activity will help you understand
your strengths, your limitations and your motivation.

Activity

Write a short letter and address it to yourself, outlining why you
happen to be considering doctoral study and what you plan to do to
succeed.

In the letter:

1. discuss why you want to embark on a doctorate;
2. outline the key strengths, skills and knowledge that you bring to
   your study;
3. identify any concerns or fears that you have regarding your study;
4. describe your tertiary educational background;
5. if applicable, describe your professional work and professional
   interests;
6. name your current scholarly interests;

> 7. describe what you hope to get out of the study;
> 8. clarify how you intend to meet the demands of high-level study;
> 9. discuss how you plan to maintain motivation for a long-term study; and
> 10. outline what you already know about doctoral study.
>
> Keep the letter in safe keeping.

Now that you have completed the activity you will be able to understand where you are coming from in the research and what you hope to get out of it. Is your motivation to understand and, perhaps, to change part of the social world? Or is it to understand and change your own personal world? If the answer is best described by the latter choice, then perhaps undertaking a doctorate is not right for you at this moment in time.

● What's research?

In everyday life it is difficult to get away from research. We are all recipients of research since we read, see and hear about research constantly through media reports, newspapers, television and other means. Some reported research provides a solution to a major contemporary challenge. Take, for example, the issue of global warming. Researchers are people with the skills and background knowledge who will be able to investigate the issue and present a way forward. But research is not simply about solving worldwide issues: minor and micro problems also present continual challenges. In sociology, for example, issues associated with migrants' employment and accommodation, isolation from family, language difficulties and so forth all need addressing. The fact is that research and knowledge discovery are important aspects of contemporary life. They are fundamental to making a difference in society.

Research in social science is a way of knowing. It is a disciplined way of coming to know something about society. Its goal is to improve the way we understand the social world. Effective research is about finding solutions and getting answers to the questions asked and advancing fundamental knowledge. Researchers carry out research when they want to know something and there is no known authority, or perhaps there are authorities but the authorities disagree. They also carry out research when they are not willing to accept without question the answers already provided. They undertake research when the existing literature does not satisfactorily answer their questions. Their questions can be answered by investigating the problem through a process of inquiry that is organised, systematic and logical.

You could be excused for thinking that there is a prescribed formula for undertaking research. Many books on research map out the process as though the steps will follow linearly and predictably. Sadly, this is not the case. Research cannot be reduced to a set of mechanical steps or a fixed, linear series of stages. There are multiple ways of carrying it out. There is no canon and there are no core methods, and hence, no consensus about how best to carry it out. To be sure, there are some technical aspects to doing research, and essential elements of the process. However, the research process is not absolutely rigid and does not necessarily proceed in an orderly fashion. Social science research is complex. There is no code of practice that applies equally across research activity. But what you need to know is that there are a number of principles that will serve as a guide.

There are many branches under the umbrella of social science research and they all focus on people, institutions and interactions. Take, for example, education, where much research is undertaken within the formal sectors and around the key activities of teaching and learning. It might involve experimental research, action research, life history, case study, feminist research, narrative inquiry, self-study, intervention research, ethnography, evaluation research, and so on. In addition it is not uncommon for doctoral students to undertake other kinds of research such as theoretical research, historical research, analytical research or conceptual-philosophical research.

The range of interests is wide. For example, in nursing, researchers might investigate areas in relation to early childhood well-being, local community health initiatives, student mentoring within a nursing programme, youth solvent abuse, migrant health professionals' professional development, and university nursing lecturers' online teaching. Each kind of research project requires different kinds of methodological tools for understanding and undertaking the task of inquiry at the doctoral level. Some of the tools used for data collection include survey, field notes, interview, document review, and using archival data. Whatever your choice, with your thirst for knowledge, you are sure to find research an exciting process.

Set out on your new journey in the knowledge that doctoral study is a unique experience. Perhaps for the first time in your life – possibly for the *only* time in your life – you will have the luxury of investigating a problem or an issue over a sustained period of time. You will be able to give your attention to the task of understanding what you think is happening. You will be able to find answers to an issue that you are passionate about or will be able to come up with solutions to a problem that you find most interesting or puzzling. With your fresh mind and fresh eyes, you will latch on to new ideas and new ways of using technology for your research. Getting started, developing the project, nurturing it, and watching it grow are all exhilarating experiences. The triumphs, the joys, the big and small achievements, all make your decision to do a doctorate worthwhile.

That's not to suggest that everything will always be straightforward. Here's what some students at different stages of the process say about doctoral study:

> *It's like sailing. I just think that I'm sailing a boat or a ship. And sometimes the sea gets really rough and sometimes it's the calm, calm sea. So it's exciting in way and it's a challenge in a way. I think that if I can maintain a positive attitude I can get through like a journey.*

> *I'm still trying to put things together. There are things that are all over the place at the moment.*

> *It's like when you drop a pebble into water and you get the ripples coming out. It kind of feels like it started off from there. I dropped the pebble and the ripples went out and got further and further apart and now they are coming back together again.*

> *The first year was like climbing a mountain. The rest of the time was being on the mountain ridge. There have been some downs and some ups but as far as the actual original climb is concerned it's nowhere near as extreme.*

> *It's like a maze. There's an entry point and an exit point and to get to the exit point you have to find your way through that maze and every now and then you'll come up against a wall. You have to find a way back.*

Students who have completed their doctorate invariably point to their personal and intellectual growth during the process. An experienced researcher, Marg Gilling (2000), has also written about the personal growth that can be attributed to involvement with research. Undertaking doctoral research deepens students' understandings not only of their area of research interest, but also of themselves. This is an important and possibly unexpected consequence. What students say is that doctoral research offers you a chance to grow. It is an opportunity to come into contact with people quite different from the ones you typically associate with, and learn from them. You might work closely with professionals, policy makers and others during the course of your research. Or you might carry out interviews or surveys with people within a specific social science arena. In these contexts you become privy to other people's beliefs, values and assumptions and discover how different these are from your own. As a result, your comfort zone is unsettled. You begin to question your own world view and way of living in the world. You begin to look at things differently. You begin to grow.

Students who have completed their doctorate draw attention to another aspect. They point out that undertaking doctoral research is a real privilege. It provides a unique opportunity to learn new tools and skills and master appropriate techniques, and to learn about and evaluate recent international advances in your chosen area. You learn *how* to think rather than *what* to think. You develop critical, logical and lateral thinking and grow intellectually. Capabilities like these provide students with the know-how to get to the core of a problem, to critique and to make links between ideas, knowledge and people. You learn to deal with complex concepts and with handling and interpreting data. You figure out where you can make a useful contribution. You start to look for the gaps in what is being told to you – the unspoken. You continually evaluate your own work in relation to current developments. Answers, comments and statements begin to come together and allow you to make connections between them.

While this may sound unsettling, you need to be clear that you will not be able to establish absolute truth about an issue or problem through your research activity. Truth is entirely subjective. It will be more appropriate for you to develop your research project around concepts such as 'rigour', 'trustworthiness' and 'reliability'. Any arguments you put forward must be based on sound evidence and should acknowledge any limitations. Your project is 'of the moment'. It is possible that another researcher in the future will produce somewhat different answers to your problem. However, your results will be important at the time they are produced. At that time comes a responsibility to others, to your discipline, and beyond. If this responsibility feels like a heavy burden to you at this point in time, then be mindful that at the end of the journey you will want to share your important findings. You learn how to communicate your findings in both informal and formal exchanges with your national and international professional research communities. By disseminating your work across the academic community, you contribute, in a small way, to understanding in the world and, perhaps, to making it a better place.

There is another aspect that students talk about in relation to personal growth. You develop personal attributes that make you a better individual. You become organised and develop systems and strategies to help keep track of literature, participants, data and so on. What's more, it is likely that you will become more patient, focused yet flexible, and understanding of others' needs, expectations and time frames. As Marg Gilling argues, research has the potential to take over your life and consume every waking moment. There are moments of exhilaration, just as there are moments of despair. But you learn the lesson of perspective. You also learn to deal with disappointments, delays, power relationships, the dynamics of trust, and the very real challenges of the unknown. Working independently inevitably brings with it loneliness. You learn to cope, you learn to trust your intuitions, you retain balance, enthusiasm and direction, and you become a stronger person for it.

Let's look at the dilemmas that researchers often face and questions that researchers ask during the early stages of research. Marg Gilling (2000, p. 18) describes these clearly for us:

> Questions are a constant: in the initial stages questions such as: What is this research really about? What do I want to find out? What if I can't find any literature about this topic? What if someone else has already done the same research? When am I going to do this research? How am I going to fit it in with ... my work, time with my friends/family, sport? ... What if no one wants to be involved? What are the ethics involved? What are ethics? So many questions, buzzing, frightening, exciting ... and present at the start of any and every new research project. Questions keep bubbling, surfacing. They may lead to procrastination, maybe a run for cover.

What you are aiming towards as a doctoral student is a thesis that will demonstrate mastery of the conventions of doctoral education. Your thesis will need to provide a logically organised and integrated account of your project. While, in some universities, it may consist of a series of published papers designated as chapters in the thesis, there must be always a sense of coherence through the thesis. The thesis will need to show that you have conceptualised, designed and carried out independent research consisting of one or more studies. It will represent a carefully planned and systematic piece of inquiry that deepens understanding. It will demonstrate that you have a sound understanding of the literature and the wider context of knowledge and the theories within which the thesis is embedded; that you have put forward a critical argument; that you have analysed your data at an advanced level; and that you have communicated your findings in a scholarly fashion.

The research must be original. Many doctoral students become concerned at what 'original' actually means. To be frank, your research is more likely to demonstrate a smaller rather than higher element of originality. If you are aiming to produce highly original research then perhaps your goal is unrealistic. Your research must also make a contribution to knowledge. It is safe to say that we cannot all offer the kinds of contributions to knowledge that, for example, Einstein was able to offer. No doctoral student should feel the need to aspire to this level. Rather, doctoral students tend to focus their efforts on producing a credible piece of research that advances knowledge in some smaller way, such as trying out something in your country that has previously only been attempted elsewhere; exploring a new area in your discipline; using methodologies typically not used in your discipline; using a theoretical approach uncommon within your discipline; providing new evidence on an issue; making new connections between different topics in your area. Our contributions are likely to be significant for a small audience and small academic community. Often it is not until the end of the project that students fully appreciate the originality of their work because it has built up slowly through the project.

Your research must also demonstrate independence. The thesis must present your own voice on the topic you have chosen. You need to detach yourself from your supervisor's voice and present your unique professional argument. Quite likely, your independence will develop from merging your understanding of the traditions and viewpoints of your discipline with contemporary literature and methodologies. If your work as a doctoral student is nested within a larger (funded) project you might wonder how you can demonstrate independence when your work 'belongs' to a team. These kinds of dilemmas need to be resolved early on, so that your research contribution is distinctive within the wider project.

There are other features that characterise a good thesis. The thesis must have a clearly defined research question or questions. These must be formulated in such a way that answers can be found. The thesis must have an aim or hypothesis that spells out what the student is trying to achieve and, relating to the problem to be investigated, it must put forward a proposition or an argument (or actual thesis). It must have ethical approval, if appropriate. It must use a research design that is appropriate to the research aim and that enables data to be collected and analysed. The thesis must draw sound conclusions from the data and should acknowledge strengths and limitations and the need for further research. It must demonstrate research competence and completeness and be written in a concise and focused writing style exemplifying a high standard of presentation in terms of grammar, sentence, paragraph and chapter construction, and consistency with the presentation conventions of tables, figures and references.

There are, then, typical stages in research. We will be looking at these stages through the chapters:

Typical stages in research

1. Planning and conceptualising the project.
        Finding a topic
        Developing research questions
        Understanding the relevant literature
3. Designing and implementing the study.
        Specifying the research methods
        Collecting the data
3. Analysing the data.
        Organising and coding the data
        Interpreting the data
4. Writing and communicating.
        Establishing the need for the research
        Clarifying procedures used
        Reporting the findings and conclusions

● Setting up for success

While we can list the general features of a doctoral thesis, there will be no formal classes to attend and no milestones to achieve while you are working on your thesis. You will be the one ultimately responsible for the work you do and for your progress. In short, the game plan has changed. Avoid getting overly anxious about this responsibility; rather, be proactive. Carry out a stock-take of your current skill set and determine where you might need assistance.

Some students like to keep a personal diary or a journal to keep track of events and schedules. This is also a good place to write down those 'brain-waves', 'inspirations' or simply 'good ideas' that you have at the time. At the end of the thesis you might be surprised at the way in which your thinking changed over time. The thesis is, in simple terms, under your management. You need to operate and manage your work differently from the approach you took in your coursework and earlier studies.

Many students thrive on the freedom:

> *"The most enjoyable thing is that I can do my own work and so I don't have to please anybody. I don't have to please my boss or my institution or my scholarship provider. I don't have to do what they want. This is my doctoral study so I do what I want."*

You should know how long you have until you are required to complete. If you don't happen to know the exact length of time, then this is a good time to start your active engagement with your thesis work by requesting a copy of the university's doctoral handbook and consulting it. Your handbook will set out the university's code of practice and will describe the mandatory practices, such as ethical compliance, responsible research practice, occupational health and safety and intellectual property. You need to be sure that you have this background information and that you know about the assistance and services that the university provides for you during your study.

Activity

Carry out some research on what your university offers you in terms of:

1. Induction programmes
2. Work space
3. Computer, printing and photocopying
4. English language support
5. Seminars and workshops
6. Online materials
7. Doctoral student association
8. Conference travel funding
9. Funding to assist with data collection and analysis
10. Student representation on the doctoral committee

Once you are fully aware of the support available, begin thinking about how you will manage your thesis work. Many students like to begin the management of their thesis work by setting out a timetable listing the activities required and a time frame for each. Let's check out one approach to developing a schedule by broad strokes. In the example provided, the first thing the student did was set the date for her graduation. She then planned backwards. At that stage she was provisionally enrolled in a thesis programme. She planned her research proposal defence towards the end of the first year. She expected that her work would require ethics approval and she built the time needed to prepare the application into her timetable. She thought that she would probably conduct interviews and anticipated that recruiting participants would take some time. Her thought was that if the interviews were to be carried out in several main cities, she needed to allow sufficient time to travel and visit her participants. She tried to allow as much time as possible to analyse the interview data, to carry out the writing and to update her literature. The key issue is that she committed herself to a clear finishing time and developed a draft plan in which to meet that end point. She was mindful that unforeseen events or difficulties might push the timeline out but she had time 'up her sleeve' if that happened.

Example: Anticipated timeline – doctoral thesis

Phase	Focus	Dates
Phase 1 Year 1	Literature review	June – October Further revision in phases 2 and 9
Phase 2 Year 1	Research design and proposal submission	Completed October Further revision possible following defence and ethics
Phase 3 Year 1	Proposal defence	November
Phase 4 Year 1	Ethics application submissions to university	January – March
Phase 5 Year 1	Participant recruitment	March – April (commences as soon as ethics approval gained)
Phase 6 Year 1	Interview data collection	April – July
Phase 7 Year 2	Preliminary data analysis	May – December
Phase 8 Year 2	Findings collation and writing up	December – May
Phase 9 Year 2/3	Discussion and recommendations	May – August
Phase 10 Year 3	Literature review update and revision	August – November
Phase 11 Year 3	Final writing and thesis submission	December – July
Phase 12 Year 4	Graduation Graduation party	December

The schedule gives the impression that the thesis will proceed in a highly structured fashion. It also gives the impression that the student will work consistently on her thesis each day. But in fact, thesis work is sometimes unpredictable and not every student is able to work under a strict time regime. Some students operate sporadically with creative bursts, working intensely for a period of time, then leaving the thesis for a while, then coming back to it when a new idea or solution comes to mind. No one approach is preferable, but you will need to identify your particular way of operating.

The larger schedule provides the big picture but is too wide in scope to work from. If you want to be structured and organised, take note of what successful students do when faced with the big tasks in life: they break the schedule down into manageable pieces. A weekly plan that sets out the week's goals as well as the resources needed to achieve those goals will be more beneficial to you than a schedule that is too global. Bite-sized tasks that can be 'ticked off' at the end of the week will put you on track for successful completion. Students invariably say that time is the critical factor in completing the thesis. Make sure you organise your time wisely and keep your weekly schedule at the forefront.

If you are intending to work on campus, be sure to find out what facilities, if any, will be available to you. What infrastructural arrangements will be offered? Will you have an office space? Will a computer be provided? Will you have access to a printer and to a photocopier? Universities typically provide specialist support services to international students, whether working on or off campus. These services provide assistance with developing cross-cultural understandings and enhancing English language skills.

"They gave me a physical work space in the doctoral students' room, but when I walked into the lab I thought I'm not going to use this because these resources are nowhere as good as what I have at home, so what's the point in using them. I had my own laptop and I wanted to use it because it was a faster model than what was there in the lab. There is also no wireless Internet access down there. So I made a decision at that point to essentially work from home and come in and use the library and so forth when I needed it.

But I found that really isolating. After that first year the Head of School arranged for me to have access to an office, and an office space made all the difference. Things really turned around from that point forward, not just because I had a physical space but I had a space that allowed me to interact with people from the Institute. I had access to people, access to resources, access to a space of my own and I think that makes a huge difference – a space where you can sit and think and it's quiet but you're not isolated. You are within a bigger organisation and I think that makes a big difference."

All students, whether based on or off campus, should inquire about their entitlements. What doctoral workshops and courses are offered? Will writing retreats be available? Will there be opportunities for conference attendance and networking with experts in the field? Will you be entitled to join in the life of your institution – for example, attending staff seminars and using the staff tea room? Will you be able to apply for research funding to help with costs such as travel to your research sites, and the transcription of your data? What grants and scholarships are available to you as a doctoral student? Which bibliographic software package does the university support? Who will pay for the software needed? What services does the library offer? Who is the person you should contact if you have any concerns about your study? Finding answers to questions like these will help you adjust to your new environment.

● Personal learning plan

There are a number of skills that will be very useful to you as a doctoral student. The first necessity is skill in information retrieval. You will need to become familiar with online database searching. It may come as a surprise to you to learn that many databases can only be accessed online. In addition, many libraries have opted to subscribe to electronic form rather than paper copies of some journals and periodicals. Computer searching is an efficient use of your time. It provides up-to-date, precise and accurate results. In addition, once you are enrolled in your doctoral programme you will have access to the university library to search the catalogue and databases. You can also reserve books and use the library webpage to check when your books need to be returned. Electronic databases allow you to search through a range of descriptors, such as title, author and subject. They also allow you to set boundaries around the search in terms of dates, language and resource type. A real advantage is that you can search online for resources any time of the day or night, at a time convenient to you.

Many students find it easier to search the university library's catalogue rather than a database for a particular journal. If your interest is less specific than a targeted journal and you want to find out everything that has been written on an issue or topic, then a database is probably the first option. Google Scholar, ERIC, Web of Science, JSTOR, Professional Development Collection, PsychInfo, Academic Search Elite, and WorldCat are all also useful databases to researchers. Doctoral students also find that Internet sites of official ministries, professional associations or groups offer useful resources for their work.

The second necessity is skill in storing and managing bibliographic references. Finding out about bibliographic software packages, such as EndNote, and learning how to make best use of them for your work is a real must. These programs allow you to:

- import and store references from library catalogues and electronic databases;
- sort and search your references;
- download and manage full texts;
- create bibliographies immediately in a variety of bibliographic styles;
- and insert citations into your documents.

Many students have admitted that spending time in learning how to use a bibliographic package is time well spent and will save you hours and hours of work later on. My advice is that, early on in your study, make a one-on-one appointment with the librarian responsible for your discipline at your university. Ask for a hands-on lesson on searching databases and on using a bibliographic package. Take time to practise your skills at your own computer. At a future time when you need further library assistance you will be able to contact this librarian directly.

Now is not too soon to start setting up templates on the computer for your work. In the first instance this could be for chapters so that when you begin your writing you will be working with the final format. Decide on your margins, font and line spacing and, if you don't already know, learn how to number pages and how to create an automatic table of contents and an automated 'List of Figures' page. All these skills will make your task so much easier. This is a good time to remind you of the importance of backing up your computer work! Creating a paper copy, copying to a data stick, copying to another computer, or any other reliable back-up will ensure that your chapters are not keeping company with many other students' chapters lost in cyber space.

Later on in the process you might want to consider learning about using statistical packages such as SPSS to organise, present and help you analyse your quantitative data. Or you might be interested in learning about software programs that will assist you in coding your qualitative data, such as NVivo®. Many universities offer courses in these data programs.

● Working on and off campus

Whether you are working off campus or on campus you will probably at some stage feel a sense of isolation. It is the nature of the work you are doing. Your university may offer residential writing retreats that will enable you to meet other doctoral students. If you are an international student and non-native English speaker, you might discover that your university offers specialist services to enhance your language skills. You may be involved in a doctoral programme that is based around a cohort of students at the same stage of work as you. Take advantage of the opportunity for intellectual interaction and the personal support that the cohort provides. The cohort will keep you motivated through the rough patches during your study. Support cohorts are sometimes established at universities for international doctoral students across disciplines. Like informal groups set up by students themselves, these formalised groups meet at regular intervals to support each other and to share knowledge and experiences. Students sometimes set up their own support with a friend or colleague who is also enrolled in doctoral study. Other doctoral students value the support of a critical friend, particularly as a sounding board for their ideas. Of course, this friend would need to have the required skills to critically evaluate your thinking. Be sure to avoid capitalising on their good will too often.

Keep up your social networks as far as possible. Family and friends are fundamentally important to your success. Avoid friendships and relationships that create ongoing tension for you and stay clear of conflict, both others' and your own. Instead surround yourself with people who support you in your work, and put yourself in a setting that is conducive to doctoral study. Some activities and interests might need to be put on hold during your doctoral study; after all, you cannot be everywhere at once. However, it is important to keep grounded, particularly when you are immersed in high-level thinking for long periods. One way to do this is to keep hold of a form of relaxation that you enjoy. It could be playing a musical instrument; it could be gardening; it could be going to the gym. Whatever you choose to continue, be sure that you allocate sufficient time in your schedule so that you do actually get around to doing it. Don't forget to eat well, stay healthy and take care of your mental, emotional and spiritual well-being. Only you will know how best to do that.

Looking ahead towards the process

In looking ahead to a successful and enriching doctoral experience, you will want to know what others have done to succeed. You will need to know exactly what standards are expected of your work. Your thesis will need to meet those standards. To find out how those standards are captured in a thesis, the best place to start is in reading other students' recently completed work. Your library will hold copies of recent theses in your discipline area.

In the next chapter we look at the topic, the research questions and the literature. The chapter guides you into formulating a research problem that is clearly and closely defined, is significant, is grounded in the literature and, above all, is able to be researched. Following on from the research problem, we will look at how to develop research questions. The chapter also helps you develop the specific skills and knowledge that will allow you to analyse, synthesise and critique the literature. It will help you to identify gaps in the research literature, so that you can make a case for conducting your own study. You will be on your way to planning and making sound decisions around your doctoral study.

Review

Main points:
- Doctoral research is a disciplined way of coming to know.
- Doctoral research is organised, systematic and logical.
- The range of interests in doctoral research is wide.
- There is no consensus about how best to carry out doctoral research.
- Doctoral research does not proceed linearly although, typically, there are a number of stages.
- Doctoral research offers students a chance to grow personally and intellectually.
- Doctoral students are ultimately responsible for their work and progress.
- A range of key skills will provide a solid foundation for undertaking doctoral research.

Key terms:
- Student proactiveness
- Thesis originality
- Thesis contribution to knowledge
- Systematic inquiry
- Critical argument
- Databases
- Bibliographic referencing

Reference

Gilling, M. (ed.) (2000). *Research: The Art of Juggling*. Wellington: Massey University.

2 Getting a Handle on the Topic, Questions and the Literature

This chapter looks at:

▶ Deciding on and then refining the topic
▶ Developing the research questions
▶ Reading widely and critically
▶ Writing the literature review
▶ Referencing

● Deciding on and then refining the topic

Doctoral study topic areas take some time to firm up. Don't be concerned that you haven't yet figured out exactly what it is that you want to study. No one expects you to have a complete project mapped out at this stage of your journey. Doctoral study is a training ground and defining your research area is a point of entrance into the research process. There are some guiding principles which, if applied to your work, will allow you to appreciate fairly quickly whether or not the topic you hope to research is manageable. Some topics appear on the surface to be reasonably manageable but on closer inspection it becomes clear that finding an answer to the problem would not be possible at all. Be clear that it takes some time to decide on a research topic and make it researchable and manageable. Of course, this can be a problem because, more than likely, this is when you really want to go full steam ahead with your study. As one doctoral student explained:

"My first year, I have to say, was the most frustrating, partly because in that first year you don't necessarily have a really good idea of where you're headed. That was the major issue: trying to find out what it is that you are going to focus on, what your research questions are going to be. But from that point forward everything seemed to slot into place. I mean, I had ongoing challenges and difficulties and things to figure out but I never felt they were insurmountable."

What we do know from what other doctoral students have told us is that your employment or your interests and experiences are likely to steer you towards a topic area. Your previous experiences in higher education might also influence the direction your project will finally take. Work and everyday experiences might well play a factor in your topic decision making but it is important to be aware of the difference between research and everyday life experience. Whilst your everyday experiences are insightful, they are always from your personal insider's view. Simply because that view is narrow in scope on account of the context of the experience, your everyday experience may not resonate with the research literature on your topic. Since everyday experience fits the particulars of a specific everyday practice it is likely that you already know the answers to, or can find solutions for, everyday issues or problems. Research practice, on the other hand, focuses on deeper under-standing. It is a disciplined and systematic way of coming to know.

Tentative topic areas tend to crystallise into something workable when they align with the literature. Simply put, you won't be able to know what to research until you have looked at the literature. Reading widely will help you clarify the research focus. As you read, unresolved non-trivial issues, specific gaps and particular areas of personal interest will begin to shine through. For example, in sociology, we might want to find out what the concept of national identity means for young people. In psychology we might want to understand the relationship between social media and post-natal depression. In education, we might want to explore the ways in which the achievement outcomes of Down's syndrome students might be enhanced. Both the reading and the revisiting of the initial research focus are crucial to the process of finally deciding on the topic. It is an iterative process: you start with a hunch of what you want to do, you read around that topic, you revisit your research focus, you read more ... until you are satisfied that you have come up with what you want to focus on in your doctoral study.

In short, reading the literature will allow you to make connections between your proposed focus and the existing debates in the field. The focus of your work will not emerge in a vacuum. Engaging with past work will enable you to tune in to an ongoing 'conversation' within your discipline that commenced long before you had even given any consideration to doctoral work. As you read the academic and professional literature you begin to get a sense of the various conversations taking place. You start to see gaps and other ways of thinking about and doing things. You begin to see how your proposed work compares and contrasts with the work already undertaken – how it expands on, makes new connections with, or explains in another way what has already been articulated. You start thinking that you might be able to mark out a place to join the conversation and consider what you might be able to contribute.

Let's be clear: reading and thinking about the literature in relation to your topic are critical stages in the planning of your research. Having a command of what is happening in your topic area will allow the focus of your study to emerge and be redefined. Not only that: your topic area will present as more far-reaching and, quite likely, more fascinating than you ever expected. In learning about what is happening in your chosen topic area, you will also learn how your topic is contextualised within the broader social landscape of policy makers, communities and so forth. You will also learn who the key figures in the field are, which projects represent landmark studies, what kinds of methodologies are typically employed, and which theories tend to be drawn upon to frame an understanding of the field. Armed with this knowledge, the places where you can make a useful contribution and how you might push frontiers become clearer. If, on the other hand, your pass through reading the literature results in a loss of appeal for your topic, find another topic. A topic that does not interest you will be unlikely to keep you going for the duration of your doctoral study.

Clarification and refining of the research problem takes time and may seem to unnecessarily delay progress with the research. But it is time well spent in the long run. Factors to consider when selecting a topic grounded in the literature relate to size, scope, time, resources, skill and access. A good research problem is one that is clearly and closely defined, is significant, is suited to the researcher's skills, time and resources at hand, and is able to be researched. Once you learn the skills of refining your research problem and making it researchable and manageable, then you are well on the way to becoming a researcher. The literature will not only help you clarify your topic; in all likelihood it will become one of the most enriching aspects of your work. Here is what one student in the early stages of her study, undertaking a professional doctorate with compulsory taught papers, says about the reading:

> **"** I love the opportunity to read widely and to look at research that I would never normally look at in my profession. I mean, it's just having access to different information that I really like. I've really enjoyed having the opportunity to explore different ideas more deeply. And you know, I hesitate to say, I enjoy the assignments and I like that the assignments make you explore ideas in a different way. Things that you wouldn't normally do.**"**

By now you will be familiar with online database searching and will have developed skills in storing and managing references using a bibliographic package such as EndNote. You may also have made time to visit a librarian at your university for an initial discussion about your proposed topic. Now you need to decide where to look further for your literature sources in order to ensure that the three main platforms are covered: the background material which will be of broad relevance to your focus, the middle-range sources which will relate in some way to your focus, and the sources very closely related to your own specific topic.

Where do you start? Many researchers begin with secondary sources such as reviews of the field, meta-analyses, literature syntheses, scholarly handbooks as well as reference materials stored in the library in order to get a broad overview of the topic. Influential authors and keywords related to the topic, as identified within these secondary sources, will assist your online search for primary sources. All kinds of literature will emerge: local, national, international, journals, reports, theses, books, policy documents, quantitative, qualitative, large-scale, small cases, early and more recent developments, different theoretical approaches, surveys, interviews, case studies and so on. Canvass as much of the relevant literature as possible – but, at all costs, keep a level perspective and avoid drowning in it. Your librarian is an important human resource in your literature searching. Information about new services, new databases and new publications, as well as information about high-impact journals and top-ranking relevant publications, comes from the librarian. It is the librarian who is often able to locate material that you didn't know existed.

Case study

Kirsten works in the policy field within the United Kingdom. She is interested in researching truancy in high schools. Her literature search began early on in her own professional work when she accessed official education documents that set out the terms of the educational contract within her country of residence. That literature led her to official documents that clarified the responsibilities of the state, the school and the family.

Following on from her document search Kirsten approached the librarian at her university for advice on where she might access literature sources. She found a number of sources that discussed the issue of student school attendance, with respect to the following social issues:

- the relationship between truant students and future employment;
- the relationship between truant students and unstructured and unsupervised activity;
- the relationship between truancy and socio-economic status;
- the relationship between truancy and students' critical thinking skills development.

Although she has not yet firmed up her research question, she is considering investigating truancy from the perspectives of school principals and school guidance counsellors.

Consider your own topic area. Once you have accessed the literature you then need to make tough decisions about the relevance and appropriateness of the literature for the purpose at hand. Not all of the literature sourced will turn out to be useful to your topic focus. You will find that the more you read, the more your focus becomes refined. Alternatively, your reading may point your work in a different direction. Another way of thinking about reading is that it will provide you with opportunities to discover where you can make a useful contribution. The point to emphasise here is that your contribution must be useful for this moment in time – not for last year, not for a decade ago, and not for the distant past. Keeping up with the literature and, through that reading, reassessing your topic area is crucial in an endeavour such as doctoral study in which the goalposts are forever moving.

A read of the abstract and a skim read of the content will fairly quickly enable you to identify those sources that do not demand your full attention. However, it is likely that many of your sources will require careful reading. Avoid copying directly from your sources. Apart from a waste of your precious time, it will not pay you dividends in the long run. Instead, what many doctoral students do is use sticky notes or highlighters – either pen or electronic – to mark those passages that are of greater significance to their work and to which they can return at a later time. Some of my students use these readily identifiable excerpts as the foundation for the notes entry of the literature source in EndNote.

Keeping track of sources demands a practical systems approach. Be sure to store the details of the literature source as soon as you have read it. In addition to entering the obvious main details – author, title, publication source, keywords – for each relevant source into EndNote once the piece is read, my recommendation is that you write one or two paragraphs that summarise in your own words the content of the literature source, in a way that makes links with your own proposed study. Students have found that these paragraphs can later be inserted, directly or without much adaptation, into their literature review. Time spent doing this will save much time later. You might store material on your database by establishing groups according to relevant themes, or, as your work progresses, according to chapters. In a similar way, store paper copies of documents, articles and the like using an organised system that works best for you.

● Developing the research questions

Research is a disciplined and systematic way of going about answering questions. Regardless of the kind of research you are planning, if you want to understand things better and find out how and why processes and practices work or do not work, then you need to carve out a topic that is researchable. It will need to be non-trivial and able to be researched, given your specific circumstances, including the time and resources you have at hand. The way of doing this within research is to pose questions which you will subsequently attempt to answer. In other words, your research questions are what you are trying to find out through your research activity. They make it possible for others to understand precisely what you plan to do and what you want to find out. They set boundaries around the topic and guide a focused research investigation. If your questions are not formulated in a way that allows you to find answers, then you will not be able to make a contribution to the topic area. The right kind of questions must be asked.

Researchers will tell you that the formulation of good research questions is one of the most important skills that a researcher needs. It is also possibly the most difficult skill required of you during your doctoral study. Researchable questions are specific and limited in scope. They narrow down the big areas that you are interested in to something much more manageable. The fewer the main research questions, the better. For example, your general area of interest might be in learning more about the effects of daylight saving on participation in sport. An area of interest like this is far too broad to guide a research study. A more limited and specific question is needed, such as: 'What is the nature of young working people's recreational sporting activities during the first month of daylight saving compared with young people's recreational sporting activities during the month before daylight saving begins?' Sub-questions that follow on from this primary research question will focus your study even further.

If you are embarking on a theoretical or philosophical research programme then your research questions will be open and exploratory. However, if in your programme of study you expect to find answers to your questions you will need to be able to gather data or evidence that can be observed, measured, touched or counted. This is what is meant by empirical research. New researchers sometimes tend to forget that it is only the observable and measurable aspects of a question that empirical research can deal with. Moral questions, as well as questions of aesthetics, fashion, etiquette, religious faith and political ideology, cannot be answered. However, with careful adjustments, these kinds of questions can be reformulated into researchable questions. For example, the question 'Is Leonardo da Vinci's *Mona Lisa* more or less captivating than Pablo Picasso's *Blue Nude*?', as it stands, is not able to be answered by research. However, it could be converted into an empirical question, such as: 'How many fourth-year students believe that the *Mona Lisa* is more beautiful than the *Blue Nude*?'

In our earlier case study, Kirsten was planning on exploring truancy. She started with the big question: 'Does truancy play a role in social development?' Constructed in this way, the question would not qualify as a research question since it requires a simple 'yes' or 'no' answer. We can make the relationship between truancy and social development, implied in the question, researchable by working through a few steps. First, we will need to be more specific about our key concepts. How will we define truancy? What period of time absent from school would legitimately be classified as truancy? In what grade(s) are our truant students? What location(s)? What is the time of year of the truancy? If you have a hunch that there might be a relationship between truancy and a specific group within the population then you might want to create further boundaries around the question. Will our truant students come from a particular socio-economic grouping? Will both male and female truant students be involved?

We apply the same kind of probes to the issue of social development. What do we mean by social development? Communication skills? Literacy and numeracy skills? A sense of cultural identity and citizenship? A sense of belonging? Contribution to social groups? Well-being? Exhibiting commonly held values, such as respect for others, tolerance, fairness? By creating greater specificity around the research question Kirsten will be in a strong position to find answers. Be aware, however, that narrowing the research question does not always mean that the question will be more easily answered. For example, 'a keen dress sense' would be difficult to justify as a measure of social development. Similarly, the category 'tall students' is unlikely to be appropriate for our truant students.

Typically, research questions evolve and shift during the beginning stages of doctoral study. In some situations you may need to change or modify them during the course of the study. However, once the research question (and any sub-questions) have finally been firmed up, it is important that your research does not stray or shift away from answering them. The methods you choose for collection and analysis of the data must match what you have determined needs to be addressed. In other words, your research needs to be fully focused on finding answers to the research question that you have developed.

Case study

Carol works in the field of health education. Within her institution, aligned with the move towards student-centred learning has been the introduction of a personal tutor model that matches an academic staff member to a student for the duration of their enrolment. The key tasks of the tutor are to monitor the student's academic progress and professional role preparation, to take an interest in their pastoral care, and to assist them with resolving a wide range of problems by directing them to an appropriate source of focused help. While the approach has been operating within specific settings for some time, the initiative is new to the health education programmes in her country. In her own setting Carol has witnessed some limitations of the initiative since its introduction three years ago. Her primary research interest is in evaluating the effectiveness of the personal tutor approach and in addressing key questions that will inform future programmes within her institution. Right now she is not sure how to go about doing that.

Case study

Annie works with students who have been identified as 'at risk'. They perform poorly in academic settings but are often successful in other fields. They are students who have been labelled as 'low achievers', 'learning disabled', 'special needs', 'low ability', 'slow learners', and so forth. Some of these students have specific learning differences such as dyslexia or Asperger's syndrome, but some simply find learning difficult. They may have behavioural problems within the classroom or other problems outside school. Annie believes that without specific help these students will leave school without the necessary skills, dispositions and knowledge to make a successful transition into the world beyond school. Improving the outcomes for at-risk students is high on her agenda. She is thinking about how she could do this through her research. Although she hasn't yet figured out what best to do, or what her specific research objective might be, the idea of working 'with' people instead of 'on' them is particularly attractive.

Activity

For either of these two case studies:

1. List a number of possible avenues of inquiry that might be sourced within the literature.
2. Develop a research question that will provide direction for the research.

● Reading widely and critically

All of us are consumers of research in nearly every aspect of our lives. As a result of research, we know, for example, a lot about the effects of smoking on health and we are also aware of some of the problems associated with poor housing. Research produces new knowledge on a daily basis. Providing more knowledge is a strong rationale for research but, as consumers, we need to interpret the research results carefully and critically to determine what that body of new knowledge might mean for us. Interpretation and critique of research is also important for your role as a researcher. Careful evaluation of the literature that is both respectful and critical, and made on the basis of informed judgements, is an important means by which new knowledge is generated and new thinking developed.

In your role as new researcher, when you begin the process of reviewing the literature you are also, in a sense, critiquing the literature. The broad reading that you have already begun will have helped you firm up your own research topic and questions. The work that you finally produce will be evaluated in relation to the contribution it makes to the wider literature. That means that you need to demonstrate not only a command and appreciation of the intellectual significance of the subject area but also your critical evaluation of the existing body of knowledge. Reading, reflecting on and evaluating the literature in your subject area are critical stages in the planning of your research. At this stage in your doctoral programme you are beginning to know quite a lot about research problems, and research questions. While you may not yet fully appreciate issues surrounding the methodology, you will at least be able to assess whether the design of a study you are reading about is appropriate for finding answers to the research question.

On the basis of your critical evaluation, you might decide to eliminate some literature from your review. Alternatively, you may decide to use your critique of a particular source as a means of strengthening the rationale for your own study. If you do not agree with a particular perspective presented in a publication, you must be able to defend your position.

The following is a list of helpful suggestions to guide you in assessing the trustworthiness of a publication.

A helpful set of criteria for assessing research	
Purpose	☐ Are the aims of the research clear?
Justification	☐ Is the rationale for the study clear?
	☐ What is the significance of the research?
	☐ What are its implications?
Prior research	☐ Has the relevant literature been examined and summarised?
	☐ Have all the issues which impinge on the topic been considered?
	☐ Is there 'a gap' in the literature which is addressed in this research?
Problem and questions	☐ Is the research problem clearly identified?
	☐ Are the research questions clear and answerable?

Research design	☐ Is the design clearly outlined and appropriate?
	☐ Will it provide an answer to the research questions?
	☐ Are instrument construction and sampling clear?
	☐ Is data analysis clear and appropriate?
	☐ Are validity and reliability considered?
	☐ Are limitations acknowledged?
	☐ Are ethical issues addressed?
Interpretation of findings	☐ Is the written description of the findings consistent with the data?
	☐ Are the interpretations consistent with the findings?
	☐ Are the research questions answered?

In essence, the critique poses the following questions of the literature source being reviewed: What was the purpose? Who was it written for? What questions were being asked? What answers were found and what conclusions were drawn? Where is the evidence? Most importantly, ask yourself: What have I learned from the review and how will I be able to use it in my work?

Students in one of my doctoral courses were asked to critically evaluate an article relevant to their topic area. The evaluation was to assess the problem, research design, research method or approach, methods of data collection and analysis, as well as results and findings. One student, who planned to undertake her research on teacher appraisal, provided the following critique of an article published in a journal.

Design aspect	**Critical evaluation**
Problem	*The problem is precise and succinct. The supporting literature is referred to in a non-specific manner. It would have been helpful if the author had expanded on the source of her research, and included a brief explanation of the origin of references such as the 'official documents' – where are these from? What does the 'existing literature' relate to? The author refers frequently to her 'current research' but does not offer any details of what the research is about.*
Research questions	*The introduction states the author is going to analyse the implementation of the reforms, yet the questions do not directly relate to this aspect, and the paper does not specifically address it.*

Methods of data collection and analysis	Non-specific research methodology. This author uses the research carried out by others to support her beliefs. Meta-analysis would give the data more credibility, as it would ensure the author hadn't inferred correlations that didn't exist. It would also be more rigorous.
Results and findings	The author has strong views formed from her research and immersion in this topic. However well supported through her reading and research, her opinions are still opinions. The original questions are not addressed in the findings.

In her conclusion of the critical review the student wrote:

> **"**I originally chose this review because in many areas the problems referred to replicate the issues that are inherent in my own country's appraisal process. The author echoes many of my beliefs about the components required for an effective appraisal programme. However, in the process of completing this assignment it became apparent that it almost certainly includes more author interpretation than I had originally believed. Critiquing this article has made me realise that my initial assessments were superficial.**"**

● Writing the literature review

As you prepare to begin your project, you will need to write a review of the literature in your chosen area. That is to say, you need to situate your proposed study in relation to the existing body of knowledge in your chosen topic area. The literature review is a crucial aspect of research preparation. It is fundamental to your work because it will allow you to build a case for conducting your study; it will guide the design and data collection of your study; it will inform the analysis of your results; and it will be drawn upon when you write about the implications of your findings. On completion of your study you will return to the literature review to establish the specific contribution your work makes to the field.

Developing the skills and knowledge to analyse and synthesise the research is the focal activity of your study before you embark on your own data collection. It is a pathway towards becoming an expert in the field. Think about the activity as intelligence gathering. It is, in effect, its own separate research project. In researching literature sources, you are probing an issue with the eyes of an eagle to view your area of research interest from all perspectives. Rather than coming up with something completely new, or already knowing the right answers, through the literature review you are trying to demonstrate through a balanced account that you are in command of what has been written on and around your topic. For example, a study on discourse on the factory floor will situate itself within the literature on general workplace discourse, and within the literature related to discourse within the manufacturing enterprise. It might cover studies that investigate duration of workers' speaking time, and duration of supervisors' speaking time. It might include discourse of shift workers at different times of the day. It might look at dialogue patterns within small groups and within two-person interactions, and it might include interactions between workers and supervisors and look at studies that have analysed in very fine detail what is said on the factory floor.

The review will show that you are conversant with the work that engages other researchers in your area, that can you identify the seminal studies, and that you have a clear understanding of the key issues and controversies specific to the area. Acknowledgement of other work greatly strengthens your argument and the sorts of sensitivities being presented with that argument. Since you cannot expect that every reader will be sympathetic to the argument you put forward, it is important that you provide sound support from the literature to ensure that you are not charged with unfamiliarity with the field. When you come to write about your study it will be in relation to what others have said, both within and beyond the discipline. Anchoring your study in the context of relevant previous research will enable you to substantiate your claims within that context.

The review will demonstrate that you have a handle on cutting-edge developments that are moving thinking forward in your area. Citing influential literature is important but you should try to avoid over-zealousness by citing every single piece of work, particularly those that are related only in a tangential way to your study. Be selective and, where you think it appropriate and necessary, justify why you chose not to review particular sources. While you might have looked at secondary sources such as summaries or reviews by others as a way into the literature, be sure to read and cite original sources.

Your review will be evaluative rather than simply descriptive. That means that, by themselves, quotations from publications will not be sufficient. Your review will offer an argued explanation of the topic, including the strengths and weaknesses of the previous studies you have found. The review will set boundaries and will locate gaps in your topic area that will point to the need for your study. It will clarify how the existing knowledge base might be developed further and how thinking might be extended further by your own proposed investigation. In a sense you are using the literature review as a way of mapping out your claim to a particular territory.

Depending on the way you conceptualise the research problem and the availability of published work, the headings you choose will act like mini-reviews to organise the literature base. You can organise the review in themes or through time periods. There are other possible ways too, such as structuring the discussion according to local or international research, or different theoretical and methodological approaches used. Whatever approach you choose, your literature review chapter will outline for readers what your topic is, and will critique the literature, both empirical and theoretical, that reports on work already undertaken. This will lead to a justification for conducting your study. An important fact to remember is that for the doctoral thesis good research is judged relative to a particular existing body of knowledge. Showing that you know the work of your professional community and are aware of the kind of contribution you will make with your research will hold you in good stead.

Now it is time to benefit from the entries you made on your bibliographic database in relation to individual literature sources. Your summary paragraphs will form the basis of each chapter. But how does one put them together?

"The literature review is quite tricky to get right. For me it's something that has been growing over time. But sometimes I find it difficult to understand what the researcher really wants to tell the readers. Sometimes I have to go through the same articles several times to understand."

Try to write a story about what has already been found. Good stories build around a plot. In the case of the literature review the plot represents your argument. Elements that are central to the argument will need to be expressed coherently with respect to that argument. In other words, you will need to show how those elements fit into the larger argument that you are presenting as your thesis. The way you do that should *not* resemble a series of disconnected commentaries or, worse, inventories and lists. You can enhance the coherence of the review by being clear as to how your references to past and current authoritative work function as filters through which you process and express what you mean. Ask yourself: Are you aligning yourself with the view presented in a piece referenced? Is there a singular view taken amongst all the references? Are the authors saying different things? What about one specific authority? Is that authority a persuasive reference point simply because he or she marks out the same territory as you? Is the view expressed by that authority consistent with another authority? Are the authors obviously right, or simply in line with your preferences? On what basis did you select the references? Parading fragments of the work of various authors will only be fruitful if you can clarify whether or not you agree with that work and identify the extent to which those references pinpoint your own position. Be up front in asserting your reasons for your position. Develop a fuller story around an authority that aligns with your position to signal how the position will be distributed across the paper.

Creating an argument is difficult work. Literature reviews that walk the reader through a succession of interesting ideas without making links demand a lot of the reader. Always make it easier for your reader by building up the central argument. Guide the reader by signposting. Have an informed view of what your reader would know already. If your work is highly novel, then you will need to be sure that your themes are presented in an introductory way. A case will then need to be made for their importance in terms that the audience can readily recognise. Connect them to the debates taking place. Rather than presenting your research as located on the fringe of debate in your chosen topic area, you need to locate it as centrally linked to current arguments. Making your research explicitly central to the debate allows you to clarify your use of terms and expressions in comparison with the ways in which these have been used in other work in your targeted field. For example, if the concept of 'relationality' is fundamental to your work, you will need to show how your use of the term is distinguished from earlier appearances of the term in the literature.

Offer a sequence of carefully orchestrated moves and stages in a way that echoes past work. Be wary of presenting too many peripheral ideas that run counter to your central argument. Take care to avoid sentences of a huge significance and moment before the reader is ready for them. Pacing is important. Refrain from giving away too much too early. On the other hand, don't be too slow in bringing your central argument to the surface of the discussion. Be explicit about the sequencing of various elements within your literature review, clarifying how each, progressively, supports your argument, so that the reader feels in command of the sequence of the thoughts expressed. Your review will pull all the various threads together, explaining and reconciling disparities, in order to create a seamless story.

Like it or not, the important point to emphasise is that the literature review continues throughout your doctoral study. You will need the persistence of a sniffer dog on the literature trail right through to the end. In actual fact, there is never an end to a literature review. But for the purposes of your project, the end point will be drawn when you submit your thesis.

● Referencing

Every time you cite other work you will need to be sure that you provide a reference to that work, both in the text and at the end in the reference list. You should not list work in the reference list that you have not drawn on in your work. The reference list is an acknowledgement of the sources that you have found useful to include in your review. It also makes it possible for others to follow up on those sources. Since the entries in the reference list form part of the evidence to support your argument, information gained from other sources without due acknowledgement may be read as plagiarised material. Hence it is vitally important that you pay referencing its due respect.

Referencing styles vary widely between institutions and individual departments. Some doctoral students may be required to use the American Psychological Association (APA) referencing style, and other students will not. Each style has its own convention for in-text citations, for quotations, for when to use '&' and et al., for reference lists and so forth.

The important point is that you need to check out at this early stage what will be required of you. If the bibliographic database you are required to use includes a facility that allows you to cite while you write in the referencing style demanded, then you will need to learn how to use this citation tool. You can find out more about referencing from dedicated websites and from the very useful book *Cite Them Right* by Pears and Shields, published by Palgrave.

In the next chapter, we look at how the researcher's world view figures significantly in all the decisions made in relation to the research. We learn that each world view has its own coherent set of ideas, values and assumptions, and each leads to different views about how the research might be undertaken. We explore the ways in which the topic chosen, the questions asked, the research methods employed, the analysis and the discussion of the findings, even the writing itself, are all directly associated with the researcher's theoretical stance. In the chapter we trace a number of major theories in social science and this leads us to possibilities when considering which theoretical position might best guide your research.

Review

Main points:
- It takes time to firm up a topic and make it researchable and manageable.
- Reading widely will help clarify your research focus.
- Good research problems are clearly and closely defined, are significant, are suited to the researcher's skills, available time and resources, and are able to be researched.
- The formulation of good research questions is one of the most important skills.
- Evaluation of the literature needs to be both respectful and critical.
- Critique is a means for the generation of new knowledge and for the emergence of new thinking.
- The literature review demonstrates your command of what has been written on and around your topic.
- Elements that are central to your argument are expressed coherently.
- The reader is guided through signposting and carefully orchestrated moves.

Key terms:
- Topic areas
- Focused research questions
- Evaluative literature review
- Thesis argument
- Referencing

Reference

Pears, R., & Shields, G. (2008). *Cite Them Right: The Essential Referencing Guide* (8th edn). Basingstoke: Palgrave Macmillan.

3 Getting Close to Theory

This chapter looks at:

▶ Where theory fits into a thesis
▶ Different world views
▶ Postmodern frames
▶ A range of theoretical approaches
▶ The place of theory in your work

● Where theory fits into a thesis

Theories are a fundamental aspect of the fabric of our lives. They allow us to understand the world more acutely. They guess at the way things are and offer ideas about how things in the world might be interconnected. Without them we would be unable to make sense of things and determine which aspects of reality are critical to us and which are unimportant. The same is true in doctoral work. The theories we use provide a lens for developing understanding. Although they are likely to be more abstract, nevertheless the theories we use in doctoral work will offer descriptions and explanations by putting into focus the phenomenon in which we are interested. Getting close to theory in doctoral study is exciting because it helps explain the phenomenon being studied. In a similar way that an optical lens improves our eyesight, the theoretical lens we use in doctoral work helps us improve our insight.

The theoretical frames we use to make sense of events and practices have consequences for how we go about doctoral work. The kinds of questions that we might ask, even down to questioning itself, stem from the sort of theories that guide our understanding about how we claim to know what we know. They are based on a set of assumptions which are often implicit, but which together offer a way of interpreting the world. Because different assumptions underpin different theories, no theory can bring everything into focus all at once. Each theory will emphasise some aspects of the phenomenon being studied more than others. That is not meant to cause alarm. It is simply to alert you to the fact that any theoretical lens prevents us from 'seeing' the details that are not emphasised.

Whatever assumptions are made, they will serve as a starting point for a formalised set of propositions that explain *why* things happen as they do. For example, we might ask: Why is the incidence of anorexia higher for high-achieving young women than for low-achieving young women? Why were employer/employee relationships in Greek tertiary institutions fraught during 2011? Why are schools reluctant to implement national standards? To help answer questions like these, a theory is put forward which provides a framework for explaining the phenomena. The theory might offer a macro-level approach to interpretation of the phenomena being studied, or it might provide a set of concepts relevant to the study and clarify specific relationships between the different concepts. In all these situations, the researcher is using theory not merely to describe the data but to build explanations about the data. Explanations are offered as a result of exploring relationships and by making comparisons. Once we can explain things, we can predict, plan for and possibly control the future.

The important point for you to understand is that social theory by itself is limiting. Equally, research data, by themselves, are meaningless. Alone, the tangible, countable and measurable features of the social world are simply facts. However, once a data set and a theory are linked together they both become meaningful and offer explanatory power. In doctoral research the two are interdependent. In order to make my point, let us consider data collection and theorising as independent, rather than interdependent, activities and see what happens. Suppose you were to provide data that revealed women over 30 years of age in the fashion modelling industry were offered fewer jobs than women in their early twenties, your report provides an interesting finding. However, it simply reports on data collection. In a similar vein, you might propose that women over 30 are victimised by an exploitative male culture within the modelling fashion industry in the Western world. If you could not support your theory with data, then your theory would be simply a hunch or speculation. However, once you introduce a relevant data set to confirm (or otherwise) your theory, then you will have moved your inquiry from unproven speculation to research activity. The point is that in research the data and the theory are truly interdependent.

This sounds as though there are definite lines of connectedness in which theory comes first and data collection comes second. In reality in the research process, the connection often tends to be circular. In particular, theory development initiates the collection of data, which, in turn, generates a refinement of theory, which may lead to further data, and so forth. Alternatively, a student might begin with data collection and, on the basis of those data, might generate a theory. Whether circular or otherwise, the process of linking a data set and a theory together is important, as is illustrated in the following vignette, where a doctoral student shares a report she received from an examiner after she had submitted her psychology thesis for examination:

"Things went wildly wrong after I discovered that one of my examiners wrote: 'The main difficulty for me is in understanding how the thesis contributes to theory. This problem starts in the introduction where the three main aims of the thesis are indicated: "describe ... describe ... describe ..." But surely a thesis needs to go beyond description? To be fair, the candidate demonstrates that there is a more analytical aim in determining the relationships between the three entities she describes. But the links to broader theory are not made explicit. Indeed, the candidate manages to discuss her "core theoretical issues" without any reference to wider theory and with no theory references.'

In research the interdependence of data and theory must be confronted. If not, the thesis will read more like a technical report than a contribution to the literature. The technical report may well expertly describe the contemporary phenomenon, but unless it explains the data it will leave little mark on the discipline's literature. The doctoral study must do something more than describe, look at and focus on, all of which are rather modest objectives. It must, instead, analyse, explain, consider in the light of prior theory, test hypotheses about, draw conclusions about, generalise to other situations, explore limits to such generalisations, or contribute to theory development.

To be more specific, in your thesis you will need to be absolutely clear about your theoretical framework. That means you will need to describe it carefully and in much more detail than through a diagram or illustration. Clarify how your framework will be able to explain the data and make predictions. Be sure that you offer a set of key concepts or constructs and show how these relate to other similar concepts. For example, a study that investigates underage drinking will, in the first place, situate the study in relation to authoritative work in the area of underage drinking. The theoretical framework developed or drawn upon, along with the literature review, should inform the data collection as well as the analysis. You will need to be specific about how this happens. Further down the track, keep in mind that if you intend to publish your work in quality academic journals, you will be expected to answer the question, 'How does this paper advance theory?'

"As with any doctorate there is always a lot of complex theory to come to terms with. I found that particularly challenging but I think that's where my supervisors have been really helpful – proactive in the sense of the sorts of things I should consider, perhaps other resources that might be helpful to illuminate areas that I might be struggling with.

● Different world views

Every theory is based on a world view. Different world views are linked to different ontological and epistemological assumptions. For example, if a tourist from the United States were to visit a remote Papua New Guinea community, it is likely that his or her Western world view would be at odds with the local community. The tourist's understanding of what constitutes the community is likely to comprise the countable numbers of people within that community. On the other hand, a member of the Papua New Guinea community might understand the community as comprising the people readily identifiable 'on the ground', together with those who have moved to other community sites as well as members of the community who have died. These *ontological* assumptions that relate to the nature of reality might be matched with *epistemological* assumptions concerning valid knowledge of that reality. The community member might take it for granted, and possibly may not be able to articulate, that he or she knows all those people are 'there' because their presence is felt in everything the community does. The tourist might defer to the seeing, touching or hearing aspects relating to the presence of community members.

In the same way, in doctoral research, the student buys into a set of assumptions that fits a particular world view. Doctoral research never happens in a vacuum. In addition to assumptions that specifically relate to the nature of reality (ontology) and to the nature of knowledge (epistemology), the student makes assumptions about methodology. To make these points clearer, all doctoral research rests on ontological assumptions about the form and nature of the reality being studied. These assumptions respond to the issue of what reality is like. The researcher also makes epistemological assumptions about what constitutes knowledge of the reality being studied. That is to say, the epistemological question concerns who can and cannot be knowledgeable and which knowledges are valued over others. Methodological assumptions about appropriate ways of developing knowledge of the reality being studied are also fundamental to the inquiry. The researcher makes assumptions based on a philosophy about the kinds of methods that might be used for studying the reality that is central to the research.

Different world views generate different theories. The fascinating thing is that theories can provide different and sometimes conflicting answers to our questions, even when the same concept is used. As an example, consider the concept of 'moving bodies'. As you will be aware, Einstein offered a world view that provided a contradictory theory to that offered by Newton. Even though the same concept of 'moving bodies' functioned in the formulations of both Newton and Einstein, the explanations offered by the theories differed markedly. The dominant Newtonian way of knowing was challenged by Einstein but, for both, it was not a question of looking harder or more closely at the data, but of different world views that framed the phenomena under study.

Different world views of research are sometimes referred to as paradigms of knowledge and are the means through which we come to understand research. That is to say, the research process, as well as the findings the research produces, are situated within and viewed through particular paradigms. They frame the way researchers 'view' the world. In particular, they communicate the key objective of the research, the way in which reality is viewed, and how the notion of truth is understood.

Positivism

Positivism is an organised approach to research based on the belief that knowledge of the world is possible. The belief is that it is possible to know what is and what is not true. Research proceeds on the understanding that there is one best way to know what is true (or not true) and that way is through a logical deductive system of rules of explanations, comprising definitions, axioms and laws. These rules, which determine which knowledge claims are acceptable (or otherwise), are independent of the social world. The positivist research process is an organised method involving precise empirical observations and measurements that are used to provide explanations in the form of causal laws to explain relationships between entities. The end point is to discover natural laws so that human activity and events can be predicted and controlled.

Positivists' view of knowledge is that it is objective, universal and true. Because everyday and commonsense knowledge is non-systematic and value laden, it is less valid and, hence, ultimately flawed. Certainty and order are important, and an explanation that is true is based on facts, precise replicable observations and laws. Thus, truth is final and values have no place. For policy makers, among others who seek certainty from research, the notion of truth as absolute is highly attractive. In this view, reality has the same qualities regardless of who is observing it. It consists of pre-existing patterns that are stable and are able to be discovered.

Interpretivism

Interpretivism is centred on the ways in which individuals and groups create and sustain their social worlds. In opposition to the positivist paradigm, the interpretivist understands the social world as so full of complexity and fluidity that it can only be investigated through a systematic analysis of socially meaningful action. To that end interpretivists focus their attention on social actors in non-experimental (natural) settings. They look at the understandings the social actors bring to events and behaviours and the sense those actors make of those events and behaviours. Their analyses involve detailed observations of people and their interrelations and interactions for the purpose of understanding, describing and interpreting the meanings that social actors, individually and collectively, assign to the social world. Their interest is also in the motives that ground constructions of the world.

Within social science, with the interest squarely on the social actor and his or her circumstances and social setting, interpretivism has become a popular paradigm for research. For example, phenomenology and activity theory are two lenses, among many others, that are currently being drawn upon for understanding socially meaningful action. The interpretivist is ever mindful that people are constantly making sense of their worlds: meanings are never static. Realities are local, specific and constructed, and, hence, everyday theories and symbols (such as language) are powerful in the, often, micro-level analyses. Values are an integral component in the meaning systems that people generate and in socially meaningful action. In that sense, truth is not absolute and certain but is socially and experientially based, embedded in fluid social interactions.

The emancipatory paradigm

This paradigm is focused on changing conditions to make the world a better place. The inquiry process is called critical inquiry. It takes the interpretivist intent of understanding the social world a step further. It does this by exposing structures, arrangements, beliefs and practices that are inequitable and that impose constraints to human freedom. The ultimate aim of critical inquiry is emancipation. That is to say, the intention behind surfacing inequities is liberation: people will be able to change their circumstances and will be able to create a more just and more democratic place for themselves in the world.

Unpacking inequitable beliefs, practices, processes and structures, and engaging in action in order to transform individuals as well as the social world, are key objectives of critical theorists. Like interpretivists, critical theorists such as feminist theorists and race theorists view reality as subjectively understood. It is not discovered but is constructed. Both interpretivists and critical theorists maintain that knowledge is a social and historical product. Their point of difference arises in the advocacy stance taken by critical theory. In advocating for specific groups, critical theory understands truth as constituting a socio-political system that requires exposure and transformation. In a sense, not only does critical theory offer a theoretical lens, it also offers a politics.

● Postmodern frames

There are other systems of thought available to frame your work. Postmodernists share some fundamental assumptions of language, meaning and subjectivity. For them, language is fragile and problematic and *constitutes* social reality rather than *reflects* an already given reality. The argument they put forward is that reality is in a constant process of construction. What is warranted at one moment of time may not be warranted at another time. Because the process of reality construction is ongoing, the postmodernist claims that there is no available access to an independent reality. There is no 'view from nowhere', and, hence, no objective truths. In their view, there is no stable unchanging world to which we have access. In addition, postmodernists claim that reason is characterised by 'local' determinants, by fallibility and contingency, and by time and place relativity. Their conceptualisation of the subject is that it is decentred, open to redefinition and constantly in process. These ideas are complex and take some time to absorb.

Like analyses of a modernist persuasion, at the heart of postmodern analyses lies an interest in understanding contemporary social and cultural phenomena. Postmodern analyses chart practices and processes and the way in which identities and proficiencies evolve, tracking reflections, investigating everyday activities and tools, analysing talk and mapping out the effects of policy, tracing lived contradictions of processes and structures, and so forth. The point of departure from modernist narratives comes from assumptions about the nature of the reality being studied, assumptions about what constitutes knowledge of that reality, and assumptions about what are appropriate ways of building knowledge of that reality.

Taken together, modernist and postmodernist paradigms offer a way of understanding the world, in general, and of understanding knowledge and truth, in particular, and, hence, of interpreting information in the humanities and social sciences. Some commentators believe that the differences from one to another are relatively unstable and are constantly in the process of change. For example, points of differentiation become less apparent in blended theoretical perspectives such as feminist postmodernism. However, for our purposes it will be instructive to view the frameworks as independent of each other.

● A range of theoretical approaches

The topic you choose for your doctoral study will sit within a discipline that tends to privilege some theoretical perspectives over others to explain phenomena. You will need to get a hold on the key theorists, the frameworks, and the terms and expressions that have significance in your area.

Activity

Consider the discipline within which your doctoral work sits.

1. Who are the important theorists in your field?
2. How are others using their work to explain findings?
3. What are the key propositions and concepts that these theories advance?

Once you have a grasp of the way theory is used in your topic area you might want to explore frameworks that are slightly outside conventional use within your discipline. The following discussion provides a range of theoretical approaches that may be of interest. The discussion includes ideas from the work of Foucault, Bourdieu, activity theory, psychoanalytic theory, sociocultural theory, and hermeneutics. Each provides a language and tools to explain phenomena. The list is not exhaustive, of course, and the aim is not to privilege any theory. Rather, the theories are offered with a view to developing your awareness of some of the conceptual tools available for framing doctoral work.

Foucault

Foucault's work (e.g., 1977) is particularly influential in the social and human sciences. Policy makers, historians, sociologists, scholars, and many others, draw on the work to analyse texts, to question what drives practices, to explore the diffusion of power and to investigate how people are caught up in regulatory practices and truth games. Their analyses highlight the complexity of social practice and the difficulty in coming up with universal checklists for explaining what we do. They show how cultural, economic, political and social factors influence processes and practices, as well as people's sense of self.

Case study

Pierre investigated how students categorised as 'slow learners' live their subjectivity in the classroom. He found Foucault's insight that discourses sketch out ways of being in the world particularly helpful. In his work he found that the discourses about 'slow learners' operating in the classroom shaped the students' thinking and practices about themselves as learners and also shaped their practices. He found ➡

that students labelled as 'slow learners' came to think and act as others expected of 'slow learners'. The discourses in circulation where he carried out his research had the effect of producing truth and, hence, they were extremely powerful.

The constructs that Pierre used to show that power produces and sustains the meanings that 'slow learners' have of themselves were 'normalisation' and 'surveillance'. Surveillance tended to make 'slow learners' want to make choices that seem 'normal' for 'slow learners'. It normalised their being, thinking and doing to the extent that they began to 'watch themselves', matching their behaviour against the standards and controls established for 'slow learners'. The practices of disciplining and regulation, he was able to demonstrate, were, simultaneously, practices for the formation of the 'slow learner's' identity.

Bourdieu

Pierre Bourdieu (e.g., 1990) provides a social field theory that allows us to understand social practice, in general, and power relations in society, in particular. His conceptual toolkit is often drawn upon to study policy, marginalisation and privilege, in general, and social class, and gender, in particular. The toolkit consists of concepts and terms, such as 'field', 'habitus', 'capital', 'doxa' and 'misrecognition'. Decisions made in everyday life (the field), in Bourdieu's view, both shape and are shaped by the capital an individual brings to the event or experience and by a set of dispositions or tendencies (habitus) that are embodied during an individual's (or a collective's) life history. Thus researchers who seek to understand the social field often focus their analyses around these key concepts.

Case study

Katie wanted to track and explain differences in behaviours, beliefs and attitudes in nursing students within the context of a formal learning environment and within the context of their practicum experience in clinics. She wanted to explain why some nurses who succeed in formal learning environments do not succeed as well in workplace environments. She used Bourdieu's concept of habitus to account for attitudes, individual nurses' dispositions and tendencies within the field of the learning environment and within the field of the clinic. Both fields contain systems, structures and relations that put boundaries around action and thinking. Both fields, she found, had their own ways of functioning.

In her study Katie found that nurses who felt at ease within one social field had a well-formed habitus, and hence a privileged position, within that field. That particular habitus, she found, was often out of place within the other field. Capital was the concept that allowed her to explore an individual nurse's 'fit' within the two social fields. It offered her the means to explain which nurses get to act, why, and how, successfully. Cultural capital was important in the analysis and was used to refer to the resources that an individual nurse brought to, or had access to, within a specific field.

Activity theory

Engeström (e.g., 1999) provides a conceptual grounding for explaining relationships between people and practices within an evolving systems network. His work is derived from Vygotskian ideas, focusing on a collective activity system as the primary unit of analysis set within a larger network of systems. Cultural-historical activity theory (CHAT) offers a way of analysing roles, responsibilities and resources in relation to a specific activity under investigation. The theory will allow you to take into account the cultural and historical basis of the communal system you are investigating, and will help you deal with change and internal contradiction within the system. Engeström has developed a model that provides a tool for describing and analysing the multiple dimensions and complex relationships between the parts of the system. The model is able to identify any clashes between elements within the system.

Case study

Jules was interested in analysing relationships and practices at a senior management level within a large manufacturing company. In his reading he happened upon discussions of CHAT. Using Engeström's model he determined that the 'object' of attention was focused on the company's production, the 'subject' was the senior management team, and the 'outcomes' were those deemed desirable for the advancement of the business. The 'rules' were those that were either implicit or articulated, or both, within the communities with which the company engaged. The 'division of labour' was that made visible between the senior management team and the production unit. 'Tools and signs' included the senior management team's knowledge and skills and the resources (human, material, technological) that were available within the company.

Using this framework Jules was able to depict the ways in which the company's production and the success of the management team were contingent on a network of interrelated factors and environments. In effect, he showed how production levels are influenced by a complex web of relationships and practices including those operating at the macro level of the company, such as government policy and procedures. He also used it to identify conflicts in terms of expectations, knowledge, and so forth, between the senior management team and other elements within the system.

Psychoanalytic theory

Psychoanalysis presents complex and well-developed theories of subjectivity. They enable us to understand the way power operates to enact the self into being, providing a particularly productive site for exploring questions of identity and change. The work of Lacan (e.g., 1977) and Žižek (e.g., 1998) provides the tools for engaging critically with the ideological frameworks through which people come to an understanding of themselves. In uncovering and exposing those engagements psychoanalytic approaches acknowledge the difficulty in capturing lived experience, the interdependencies and forms of obligation and reciprocity, and the place of emotions that shape those engagements.

Case study

Anton's project explored the identities of teachers in their first year of teaching in schools. He drew on the psychoanalytic framework of Žižek to show that beginning teachers are caught in a never-ending attempt to capture an understanding of the self. Narratives of the self that the teachers offered, he found, were constructed in relation to the culture in which the self was lived, as a fantasy of how others might see that self. With these ideas, Anton was able to identify a trace of misrecognition that arose from the difference between how one party perceives itself and how the other party perceives it.

Anton noted that this process of self-construction was continuous. For example, he demonstrated that many teachers worked hard to construct a sense of self-as-teacher that played out as attention to official curriculum documents, to the policies and directives within the schools in which they worked, to emphases placed in the teacher education course, and so on. Anton's use of the psychoanalytic framework highlighted what often escapes expression but what can be construed from the psychical dynamics at play within any social setting.

Socio-cultural theory

Socio-cultural perspectives draw their inspiration in part from Vygotskian ideas. Vygotsky (e.g., 1978) proposed that the origins of thought are entirely social and that conceptual ideas necessarily develop from the intersubjective to the intrasubjective. The theory has created much interest particularly amongst developmental and cognitive psychologists. In the theory relationships between the individual and the social, and the cultural and historical context are highly significant. To that end, Vygotsky's formulation of the social construction of knowledge endeavours to make links between culture and knowing by prioritising shared consciousness, or intersubjectivity. The focus for a wide range of socio-cultural analyses is on representation and mediation. Semiotic mediation theory is proposed to account for intersubjective arrangements and the part those arrangements play in the development of internal controls in the development process.

Case study

Janice investigated second language learning in an adult evening class over one year. She was drawn to the Vygotskian understanding that language develops in a kind of apprenticeship context in which a learner gradually comes to follow and mimic a more experienced or capable knower and, in time, is able to model, by him- or herself, the language activity. Tools such as linguistic constructs act as mediators. She used Vygotsky's concept of the zone of proximal development (ZPD) to explain development that is not yet fully mature. Her use of the concept focused on the difference between what an individual can do with and without assistance.

In Janice's investigation the second language students enhanced their learning as they increased their participation in the evening class and by being scaffolding in experiences that lay within the zone of proximal development. She was particularly interested in the part that the peer community played in that development. The social environment of the peer community and the role of language development within that environment created a particular social context for second language development. In her study Janice found that peers acted as coaches and as co-creators of the learning culture, and were able to mediate between the printed and spoken word and the learning effectively.

Hermeneutics

Hermeneutics is understood as the theory of interpretation of meaning. The hermeneutic perspective is based on a philosophy that conceives of understandings as in constant movement. Gadamer (e.g., 1975) argues for an interpretation of lived experience that emphasises understandings as states caught in ongoing formation, rather than as a fixed reality. Experiences evoke different meanings for different people, and are informed by culture, tradition and the context in which they are developed. Any understandings that emerge are based on a shared consensus which is fluid and never final. The development of understandings also emphasises a circularity referred to as the hermeneutic circle.

> William's overriding interest was in technology and in how people create understanding through digital media. He was drawn to a hermeneutic framework to explore how learning takes place within online environments. His research setting was a class of tertiary students who were based in a range of geographical locations and who received their instruction through synchronous multimedia conferencing.
>
> He used the concept of the hermeneutic circle to describe how an individual develops explanations based on his or her interpretations of the phenomena within the lesson. These explanations then encounter resistance from broader discourses, so that the individual's understandings evolve and the explanations shift. The circularity between present understanding and shifts in explanation, in turn, evokes a new understanding. As the interpreter's attention moves cyclically from the part to the whole, to the part and so forth, some resolution or consensus will emerge. That is to say, through cyclical engagements with the phenomena, individuals draw forward their pre-existing knowledge from prior experiences. As this occurs, their understandings become further enriched from new, evolving perspectives. As the individual re-engages with the learning task from these fresh perspectives, understanding evolves.

● The place of theory in your work

As you read through the previous section, one theory or another might have sparked resonance with your work. If not, then keep searching through the literature and keep an open mind.

> *"Getting your head around all the theory and then trying to work out which one is really the theory that you most engage with or is most relevant, you know, really did take some time. Once I'd identified the theory, everything else fell into place. But you know there was a lot of reading and a lot of talking to people. I guess using those networking skills helped but it did take a while for me to identify that theory."*

Remember, above all, that what you are ultimately seeking to do is use theory as a sharp instrument for interacting with the data at a level beyond mere description. You might find that a single theory is not able to account for every aspect you want to investigate. One student I know blended her analysis with theory drawn from the work of both Foucault and Lacan. Her thesis offered a Foucauldian analysis, exploring the operations of power in an institution, and a Lacanian interpretation that explained the effects of that power on individuals' sense of self.

This is a good time for you to begin the serious task of firming up on the theoretical framing of your own work.

Activity

Consider the main objectives and the research questions of your proposed work.

1. What are the key constructs/terms/concepts relevant to your work? (For example, systems/identity/meaning making/relationships ...)
2. Write down the possible theories that would help you explain and analyse those constructs in the way that you anticipate they will operate through your work.
3. Make a decision on your theory of choice.

In the next chapter we take our focus off theory to explore research designs. However, the theoretical underpinnings of research will influence the ways in which the research is carried out. We will look at a range of methods and strategies used in social science research. While most research is empirical research, it is not uncommon for doctoral students to undertake theoretical research, analytical research or conceptual-philosophical research. Each requires different kinds of methodological tools. We explore the more common research methodologies and look at what is involved with specific research methods.

Review

Main points:
- A theoretical frame provides a lens for developing understanding.
- When a theory and a data set are linked they become meaningful and are able to offer explanations.
- Every theory is based on a world view, and different world views are linked to different assumptions.
- World views are referred to as paradigms of knowledge.
- Theoretical lenses communicate the key objective of the research, the way in which reality is viewed, and how the notion of truth is understood.
- It is important to be familiar with the key theorists, concepts and propositions in your topic area.

Key terms:
- Ontology
- Epistemology
- Paradigm
- Positivism
- Interpretivism
- Emancipatory frames
- Postmodern frames

References

Bourdieu, P. (1990). *In Other Words: Essays Toward a Reflexive Sociology.* Trans. M. Adamson. Cambridge: Polity Press.

Engeström, Y. (1999). Innovative learning in work teams: analysing cycles of knowledge creation in practice. In Y. Engeström, R. Miettinen and R.-L. Punamäki (eds.), *Perspectives on Activity Theory* (pp. 377–404). Cambridge: Cambridge University Press.

Foucault, M. (1977). *Discipline and Punish: The Birth of the Prison.* Trans. A. Sheridan. Harmondsworth: Penguin.

Gadamer, H. G. (1975). *Truth and Method.* London: Sheed and Ward.

Lacan, J. (1977). *The Four Fundamental Concepts of Psycho-analysis.* London: Hogarth Press.

Vygotsky, L. (1978). *Mind and Society.* Cambridge, MA: Harvard University Press.

Žižek, S. (ed.) (1998). *Cogito and the Unconscious.* Durham, NC: Duke University Press.

4 Getting Designs on Methods

● Research designs

Doing research is an exciting activity. For a start, you have already got to know a lot, simply from your engagement with the literature. You have already made a number of important and exciting decisions: you know what you want to research and you know what research questions will guide the direction of your work. You also know the world view that will frame your work. Now it is time to talk about research designs.

In developing your research questions and in couching your work within a specific theoretical frame, you have already prepared the ground for thinking about the kind of research design required. Let's think about the research design in the same way as we think about the design of a house. It is a plan. It is systematic and logical and it is guaranteed to make the building stand firm. The owner might have commissioned a design for any number of purposes. For example, it might be a building plan for a holiday house, or a large family home, or an apartment. It might be a plan for a factory. It depends on the owner's purpose for the building. In the same way, your research design will fit the purpose of your research. Different purposes initiate different research designs, and, if the fit is good, your research design will hold your research together.

Not only do different purposes initiate different designs, different special requirements also lead to design variation. Let's return to our building plan. There are many possible designs for buildings of the same purpose. Before the plan can be drawn up for a family home, for example, the owner will have addressed fundamental questions concerning the family's needs for the home. The specific requirement in terms of the number of levels of the house, the number of bedrooms, the approximate size of the living space, and so on, all need to be addressed. There are finer details, too, such as the location of the refrigerator in the kitchen, and the owner will need to make a decision on these as well.

In the same way, a research design for the same purpose will vary in the detail. Before the design can take shape, questions ranging from the broad to the specific will need to be addressed. Let's begin with you first. Are you fascinated more by numbers, historical documents, ideas or people? Your answers will influence your design. Now let's turn to the research questions. What data will need to be collected, from whom and where and when? How will the data be collected and analysed? When you make these decisions with careful thought, your design will provide a coherent plan for undertaking the research. It will demonstrate a conceptual integrity between the purpose of your research and your decisions concerning the information and data needed, the ways in which you will collect and analyse the data, the numbers or kinds of participants in your study, and how you will report the findings.

The decisions that you make in your design are not to be taken lightly. They will influence the kinds and level of findings you make and, hence, will significantly influence the conclusions that you are able to draw. If constructed carefully and rigorously both at this stage and iteratively through the data collection and analysis process, the research design will not only offer a logical plan for your research, it will also supply you with appropriate and adequate evidence to answer your research questions effectively and efficiently. It will guarantee that your research will stand up to scrutiny.

● Research design purposes

Different designs develop from different research purposes. Each provides a structure to allow specific kinds of questions to be addressed. Some researchers are interested in understanding some thing or some people, and in fathoming out what is going on. Some are focused on solving a puzzle and finding a solution. Others are more interested in theorising and in explaining things in a new way. Still others are keen to change and improve a situation and in researching how that might happen in collaborative activity. Some want to explore differences in events over time or through precise experimentation.

The fascinating thing is that every research purpose asks a different kind of research question. What is going on? What is the solution? How can this be explained more clearly? How can this be improved? How effective is this? Each kind of question provides direction for and sets limits on your research. Each also points to a different kind of research design. This is an opportune time for you to address the purpose of your research.

Once you have identified the specific purpose of your intended research, the research design that will allow you to address your research questions will become clearer. If you are keenly interested in understanding some thing or some people, and in working out what is going on, your design orientation may well be case study and/or ethnography. For example, a researcher might be interested in finding out how students experience empathy in an online nursing course. The researcher might explore the experiences of the students and perhaps the lecturer within one class, which would then become the 'case' to be studied. A truly ethnographic study of this case would require the researcher's direct observations of what the online experience of empathy might be for the students and the teacher over a sustained period of time.

If your interest is in solving a puzzle and finding a solution, then you might be also be drawn to a case study design. For example, suppose your interest was in community sport and recreation and you were interested in developing facilities that meet the present and future needs of the local community. Your local community would become your 'case', and your research might centre on understanding their sport and recreation needs and their views of the current and proposed facilities.

Thinking carefully through your research purpose, objective or aim will help clarify your research orientation. If theorising and explaining things in a new way is your objective, then you will have a more theoretical or philosophical orientation. If you want to change and improve a situation, your orientation is likely to be action research. Let us imagine that your interest is centred on improving workplace systems in a way that is more responsive to technological innovations. You might research the development and change of workplace practices over a period as they are facilitated systematically by a change agent.

If exploring differences in events over time is of primary interest, then you might be drawn to an historical or longitudinal design. For example, you might want to explore the effectiveness of different local-body voting systems in your area over a 20-year period. Financial costs and voters' experiences might be two factors that you explore. If the evaluation of a new initiative is your objective then you might be drawn to an experimental design. As an example, you might want to evaluate the effectiveness of a new adult reading programme offered to new settlers in your community. You might assess the difference in effectiveness between a current reading programme with one group of adult readers and a newly introduced reading initiative with another group of adult readers.

Each of these research purposes generates a different research design. Each design, in turn, provides a possible structure to allow specific kinds of questions to be addressed.

● Research methodology

Designs do not simply arrive out of thin air. They are built on theoretical foundations which we will broadly name here as positivist, interpretivist or emancipatory. These different standpoints shape the way reality is viewed and the way in which the notion of truth is understood. Each provides a framework and a grounding for the way in which the study will be conducted. In the examples above, a positivist framework is associated with the experimental design of the adult reading programme; an interpretivist framework is linked to the ethnographic design of the empathy study; and an emancipatory framework is associated with the action research design of the workplace study. We can think of each of these frameworks as giving direction to as well as grounding the study. This is known as the methodology. It influences the nature of the research design and, as part of that, the gathering and the analysis of data.

Designs founded on positivism are generally known as quantitative research designs. They involve both intervention and non-intervention research and include experimental research, correlational research and survey research. The design follows a linear, sequential and deductive process for proving or disproving hypotheses. That is to say, quantitative designs are in the business of testing theories. They look at facts, numbers and measurement and focus on convergences as well as variation within a specific dimension or variable across and within a given population and situation. Their methods enable the 'impartial' and 'detached' researcher to investigate a wide range of areas but typically more at the surface level rather than in depth. Experiments and closed questionnaires are examples of what might be used in such designs.

Let us suppose our interest was in female CEOs in very large companies in the United States. We would be interested in the number of these people, the age of the women, where they were located, what their work entailed. A quantitative design would allow us to find out those details. We might decide to use an online questionnaire and post it to all very large companies across the United States. We would need to be sure that the scope of the questions in the survey was sufficiently broad to allow us to gather the information we were particularly interested in, since all the data would be collected in this one instance. From the data we would be looking at patterns that could be generalised and from which we could make predictions for the future. Our analysis would offer a broad, yet necessarily shallow, overview of female CEOs in very large companies. We would be able to report similarities in the demographics, and converging of work experiences of the female CEOs. In statistical terms, we would be reporting measures of 'central tendency'. We would also want to report on variations within the data. These data are known as 'measures of dispersion'.

Designs based on interpretivism are known as qualitative research designs. They include explorations of cultures, people and individuals. The purpose is to look in depth at what is going on holistically, in an evolving and circular way. The focus, then, is on 'texture', in exploring how separate parts and their interconnections contribute to a cohesive entity. Interpretivist designs are drawn upon for a wide range of studies, from the highly theoretical to the deeply empirical sociolinguistics study of conversations. Whatever the format, these designs are inductive and do not rely on numbers or measurements. Interviews, diaries and focus groups are sometimes used as data collection methods in these designs. Interpretivist designs may also be founded on emancipatory principles.

As an example of a qualitative design, let us look again at our study of female CEOs in very large companies. Suppose we were interested in the past work experiences of the women and in the ways in which those experiences contributed to their current positions. We would be looking closely and intently at influences in the development of female CEOs. We might opt for individual interviews with a small group of such women, with the understanding that the researcher's involvement in the interviews is not impartial. As information during the interview is shared by individual participants, the researcher may explore new lines of inquiry. It is likely that each narrative from the women will be unique; therefore, generalisation of experiences to the wider group of female CEOs may be difficult. However, the report we produce will celebrate diversity and difference, offering rich insights from the working lives of individual women.

Mixed method research designs combine both qualitative and quantitative research procedures. Data from the separate designs are integrated or mixed. When used in social science research to study human phenomena, they are offered at both the level of overall inquiry design as well as at the level of data collection methods. Their use might involve a mixed design such as in the use of survey design combined with a case study design or an action research design. With regard to methods, it might involve the use of quantitative procedures to gather and analyse numerical data and the use of qualitative procedures to collect and explain descriptions of human behaviour. Typically, when the mixed methods design is used to represent human phenomena in social science research, open-ended interviews and/or unstructured observations are offered to provide a complementary voice to questionnaires.

For example, our study of female CEOs of very large companies might incorporate a mixed methods design which pairs a national survey with individual interviews from a representative sample of women. The survey provides baseline quantitative data from multiple and varied perspectives and the interviews offer perspectives given at a deeper level. The researcher then merges the two sources of data together. The researcher will have several purposes in mind and might justify the design's use on the grounds of greater generalisability of findings, stronger validity or credibility, more reliable triangulation of data, as well as a deeper and more comprehensive understanding of human phenomena, perspectives and values, and greater insights into the social world.

A range of designs

Ethnography

Ethnographic designs represent procedures for writing about people. The term 'ethnography' is now applied to a range of studies, typically requiring the researcher's direct involvement with a group in its natural setting. Ethnographic studies are founded on the notion of people as meaning makers. Such studies emphasise that what people say and do are informed by the meanings they construct, in collaboration with others, of their cultural world. The focus, then, is on understanding the complex and dynamic cultural world. In particular, the interest is on personal and social realities, that is, on how people interpret and use their everyday worlds. Ethnographic studies engage with the qualitative design purposes of developing theories. They are not concerned with testing established hypotheses. Honouring the participants' agency in meaning making, such studies use a variety of data-gathering procedures, such as prolonged observation of the setting, document and artefact analysis, and interviewing members of the culture, and draw on the group's historical context as a backdrop to find out and document in-the-moment as much as possible about the group's everyday life. But the design is not likely to be fixed at the planning stage since new interests may emerge that initiate new lines of inquiry or a sharpening of focus as the research proceeds. The researcher's decision making regarding data collection is necessarily in a state of flux but will be informed by the kind of data hoped for in the analysis.

Case studies

A case study has no single universal design structure. Like ethnographic designs, case studies use a range of methods and data sources for understanding human phenomena. Case studies focus attention on a 'case' – one individual, one group, one setting, an activity, or an issue – to learn more about the phenomena under investigation. As with ethnographic designs, a case study design involving participants provides them with a voice and a power as experts in the setting. Factual information is typically enhanced with the views of participants for a deeper interrogation of the phenomena being studied.

Unlike ethnographic designs, the case study design may be informed by either quantitative or qualitative design purposes. A case study design might employ only quantitative procedures such as 'objective' observation, or analyses of survey, archival or systems data to test a theory about the case. More likely, however, in social science research, and depending on the resources available and the boundaries established for the research, the design might use a range of qualitative procedures in order to emphasise the social construction of meaning. It may also involve mixed methods to identify, describe and analyse in detail the complexity of the case, before determining the fit or otherwise with an existing theory and existing relevant literature. Whatever the procedures used, the point is to understand the case more deeply, rather than to make more general claims that could be applied beyond the case. However, while the findings may not be generalisable more widely, they may be suggestive of what is happening within the population at large.

Action research

Action research designs are action plans for emancipatory purposes. The designs map out systematic procedures to solve real problems and to effect change and improvement. Action research is collaborative research undertaken *with* people rather than *on* people. While it can take a number of forms, it will begin with a problem or an issue within a setting and involves the people within the setting working through a process to bring about a change and a new vision. The highly structured process is developed from the understanding that ready-made solutions are inadequate to deal with the complexity of human behaviour and to initiate long-term change. More often than not, the researcher works in collaboration with the group to facilitate change within the setting.

As with case study designs, action research designs may be informed by either qualitative or mixed methods design purposes. Although the researcher and the participants may have a clear plan of the current and proposed situation, the approaches taken to shift from one situation to the other are not fully within the researcher's control. The design will be adapted through a series of cycles or spirals that slowly advance action and behaviour in the setting towards the intended goal. In a sense the design is a plan for trial and error: planning, action, observation, evaluation, re-planning, action, and so on. More specifically, the cycles begin with a clear identification of the problem, and a shared understanding of 'where we are at and what needs to be done', taking into account the available resources and the time frame. Data collection and analysis and evaluation of the situation will then lead to the development of new theorising to inform further action and further cycles.

Experimental and non-experimental designs

Experimental designs are quantitative procedures used to investigate the effect of an intervention. It is an exploration of what happens when one variable is systematically manipulated over another variable. The one manipulated – the independent variable – is known as the experimental treatment, and the one observed is known as the dependent variable. If, as a result of the intervention, outcomes change more than merely by chance, then we say that a causal relationship exists between the two variables. Let us look at an example to illustrate. Suppose you were interested in the effects of teaching the 'times tables' by a new method. One class in a school was taught by the traditional method, and another, equally matched class in the school was taught by the new method. Both classes sit the same test after their respective units of work on times tables. You then compare the results, and if there is evidence that your new method produces higher results then you could conclude, within certain limitations, that the new method is more effective.

Non-experimental designs investigate relationships among variables, rather than manipulate them. Designs that use statistical analysis to determine the relation or association between variables are known as correlational designs. The most commonly used non-experimental designs are survey designs. Survey designs include questionnaires, structured interviews, documents and structured observations and each is used to collect data from people at a given point in time. Although survey designs are situated among the family of quantitative designs, they tend to be more exploratory in nature. They are used in order to provide a broad picture or a statement of trends to do with characteristics, features, attitudes, opinions and behaviours of people.

Narrative research designs

Narrative inquiry is focused on personal experiences. Informed by qualitative purposes, narrative research designs provide the researcher with the means to write about the experiences and lifestyles of individuals or groups over a period of time through the stories narrated to them. Such designs are particularly influential in research into social change since the data sources gathered offer unique perspectives of the social event under investigation. In these designs, because the theoretical perspectives or frames of references of the participants may well be different from the researcher's, there is a pressing need to make explicit the position of the researcher within the research activity. In some narrative inquiry designs the focus of the research is squarely on the researcher and his or her own personal experiences.

In narrative research designs personal experiences are recorded systematically using both traditional and contemporary methods through the use of artefacts, video diaries, interviews, journals, letters and so forth. There are a number of issues that demand attention and these relate to the issue of storying oneself through time, and the problem of accounting for historical events. In addition, the economic and cultural context for the story needs to be made explicit. Then there is the issue of reflection. What does the storyteller choose to say and what does he or she choose not to say? There is also, for the researcher, the issue of emotions to confront and how the storyteller articulates feelings and dreams.

Historical research designs

Historical research at the doctoral level is both descriptive and analytical. It not only describes events and behaviours, it also offers a critical interrogation. The purpose is to learn from history in order to fill a gap in our knowledge and, often, to understand the present. Historical research does more than offer facts and figures; it offers a story about the past that involves social, cultural, and, possibly, emotional experiences. As with narrative inquiry designs, historical research is highly interpretive and hence is informed by qualitative underpinnings in relation to the construction of social, cultural and political meanings. Interpretation operates at a number of levels including what material the researcher chooses to select or reject as data and the ways in which the data are constructed in the write-up of the history.

The historical researcher works with primary and secondary sources of material and aims for accuracy, authenticity and completeness. Primary sources offer first-hand public or private evidence of the phenomena being studied. Multiple primary sources are often drawn upon by the researcher and these include interviews with key informants, letters, official documents, archival material, emails and journals, even down to the sketchy notes of those directly implicated in the past event under investigation. Secondary sources add depth to the study by offering material from biographies, newspaper reports, commentaries, and so on. All these sources need to be interpreted and constructed in a critical way so that a fuller picture may be provided and better insights may be offered into the historical event.

Grounded theory designs

Grounded theory designs are further examples of designs based on interpretivism. They are systematic qualitative procedures for exploring people and processes. The objective is to draw on the perceptions of people in order to generate a theory that might explain what is going on in a holistic way. More precisely, the researcher analyses the data inductively and this leads to new associations amongst concepts and new questions which, in turn, lead to additional data collection. The iterative process results in the generation of theory. Grounded theory, then, is a theory grounded in the perceptions of people. Although they have their own design purposes, both ethnographic and narrative research are sometimes considered as examples of grounded theory designs.

As with the researcher involved in action research, the grounded theory researcher may have a plan for the research, yet the design is more likely to emerge as a result of careful reflection and evaluation of the initial data gathered and analysed. Typically, the design procedures that the researcher uses involve observing and interviewing and categorising data according to themes. Once the data are interpreted, they may be represented in the form of diagrams or models as a means of explaining the theory.

We have looked at a number of possible designs for research. Since there is a wide range of design options available to you, you will need to be sure that the overall design you choose will allow you to address your research questions.

Activity

Consider again the research you are hoping to do.

1. What overall research design would enable you to meet the key purpose of your research?
2. How will your chosen design help you meet the key purpose of your research?
3. Why have you not chosen any of the other designs described above?

● Data collection methods

The research design you have chosen will steer you towards the kinds of sets of data that will enable you to address your research questions. Since there is a wide range of data-gathering options available to you, you will need to be sure that your chosen methodological track will generate appropriate and reliable data. It should also ensure that your data will be of sufficient quantity and of suitable quality for your analysis. There are no hard and fast rules about the kinds of data you should gather for any given design. However, different research designs tend to lend support to specific kinds of data sets. Suppose your topic area was nursing practices in the battlefield during the First World War, then your historical research design would suggest you need to access patient records, archival documents and historical camera footage, and so on.

By now, it should be clear which data types would not be appropriate. In the wartime nursing example, it is unlikely that you would want to carry out observations or use video to gather your data. Similarly, if you were evaluating a new nursing instructional method, it is likely that you would be more interested in data relating to nursing students' test results and perhaps students' perceptions following the application of the method than you would be in gathering archival data. The methods you choose to collect your data will depend on what you want to find out and who you want to find it out from. The data collection methods most useful to you are those which provide direct access to the phenomenon you are studying. Sound methodological decisions create a strong logical flow within your research design. They enable strong connections between the methodological framework and the methods of data collection and data analysis, ensuring that the design is reliable, rigorous and valid for addressing your research questions.

You will also need to confront the issue of the scale of the project and the resources you have available – both material and time. Addressing these questions systematically will help you avoid under-collection or over-collection of data. Without careful thought and deliberate planning, it will be too easy to overlook an important data source. It will be too late at the analysis and writing stages of your workplace study, for example, when you realise you should have interviewed the team manager as well as the team, or when you become aware that you neglected to ask the team an important question. Similarly, it will be too easy to become distracted in the field so that you end up collecting superfluous data that stray into 'interesting' other research areas. Much as you might justify collecting this set of data on the basis that it might come in useful, remember to keep your research questions squarely within focus. A focus on the research questions will help you make the really hard decisions concerning the most useful and critical data that will provide convincing and reliable evidence.

While you are attending to the issues concerning too few and too many data sources, you need to give due consideration to the answers you expect from your research question. Then ask yourself how you plan to analyse the answers you expect to collect. This point is important because the decisions you make concerning your data analytical tools will influence the kind of data you need to collect. A common mistake amongst doctoral students is in trying to figure out what to do with the data *after* it has been collected. Ask yourself early on: what kind of data will yield the response I expect to get from my research questions, and how do I propose to analyse that data set?

Case study

Kieran has sound personal understanding of the work of an assistant principal in a secondary school. He has been one for a number of years. He gets immense satisfaction from his job and has no strong desire to 'move up the principal ladder'. He wants to know what others in the job feel about their work. However, he is not so much interested in what they think about and what they do in terms of the managerial, organisational and disciplinary aspects of the job, but on their views of the role they play in instructional leadership.

He has a hunch that many assistant principals are not given significant opportunities to provide instructional leadership at their schools. He wants his research to create a clearer picture of the role of assistant principals. In particular, he wants to find out about the professional challenges they confront and the support they receive in undertaking their role, and, importantly, the perception they have of their impact on improving teaching and learning in the schools they serve.

He is not certain yet how big his study should be. For example, he is not sure how many assistant principals the research should include; nor is he clear about the geographical and socio-economic locations his research participants will come from. Should he focus in depth on a small number of participants or should he broaden the study? These are the big decisions facing him.

As in Kieran's case, there are a number of big decisions relating to your data collection that you face. Suppose, for example, your design was experimental and you were interested in the effects of a new teaching strategy in the classroom. However, you wanted to be sure that student aptitude was controlled for in the experiment so as not to distort the effects of the teaching strategy. You might decide to use a standardised, already established instrument such as a scholastic aptitude test to provide you with students' scores. A reliance on standardised *instruments* is a common practice in quantitative designs.

Other designs rely more on self-developed *protocols*. For example, in finding a solution to the problem of the types of recreation facilities required in a local retirement village, you might expect, given the mobility restrictions of these people, more sedentary activities to feature high on the requirement list. Of course, you would want to ask the elderly people themselves for their views on their recreational needs. A needs assessment might be undertaken through a survey to gauge the community's needs. The assessment might also be undertaken through individual or focus group interviews. Or, you might use both survey and interviews. Do you have the resources and skills to develop and analyse a survey and interview data? Will the analyses provide you with answers to your research questions?

"What I needed help with most was with my survey – both assistance with putting it together so that it is going to be meaningful and assistance with the whole analysis. When it came down to it I realised that I just had to do it. I had to learn how, so I learned how to use SPSS and used some tutorials from the manual. At the same time I bought some qualitative software for myself and I learned how to use that for my focus group interviews. The quantitative stuff, it was self-taught. The qualitative stuff was more satisfactory because my supervisor had used that particular software herself and that meant I had a support mechanism."

In addition to survey and interview, the methods of data collection that are available in social science research activity also include observation as well as non-obtrusive methods to gather the data sources from government, agency and archival records collection, the Internet, newspapers, magazines, artefacts, and so forth. Data tools are those that assist with the data collection. These include questionnaires, focus groups, tests, observation checklists and records, interview schedules, written, audio and video recordings, and journals. You might want to combine the tools and use a questionnaire for a broad understanding of your topic area, and interviews to find out in more depth about your area of interest. Adding observations at the research site to the mix will provide you with the means of triangulating and verifying the data.

Let us look briefly at these three methods of data collection. *Survey* methods aim to capture attitudes, values, behaviour, preferences and the like, at a point in time. You will be well familiar with the survey consisting of a series of questions, usually relating to an issue, administered online, through postal mail or telephone, or in person. There are a number of considerations for the researcher to address. First, if a questionnaire is used, practical considerations such as user-friendliness in terms of presentation, instructions, language, tone, layout, space for responses and so on are all highly important. It is advisable to trial the questionnaire through a pilot study. Second, the questions, and the order they appear in the questionnaire, need to be thought through very carefully. Be warned that the questions will take you longer to develop than you anticipated. Third, if you are surveying a group from the wider population, your sample will need to be generated through appropriate sampling techniques in order for you to generalise your findings to the wider population.

Interviews are a means to gaining an in-depth understanding of the human phenomena being studied. They may be conducted with individuals or with focus groups of people. They may consist of structured, unstructured or semi-structured formats. Unstructured interviews offer flexible approaches to interviewing by allowing the participant to shape the content of the discussion. It is a particularly useful approach when exploring a complex domain, or when the domain is not well known. Structured and semi-structured formats guide the participants' discussion more closely. In focus group interviews the researcher acts as facilitator, aiming to elicit a wide range of views, to provide participants with greater thinking and reflection time, and to gain more insight from the group's interaction than might be possible through individual interviewing. The researcher needs to be alert to power and cultural issues within the group and needs to ensure that the group's interaction remains evenly balanced. In both individual and focus group interviews, the interviews may be audio or video recorded or may be recorded through notes or checklists. A recording check is essential, as is a brief pre-interview familiarisation meeting to establish rapport, trust and confidence with participants.

Observations are data collection techniques consisting of either structured or unstructured formats. In quantitative research designs the observation is recorded on highly structured schedules that categorise behaviours into small segments over equal time units. In qualitative research designs, observations are unstructured in the sense that the observer is listening and looking for more general behaviours that represent responses to bigger questions. The observations are typically recorded through field notes or video files. They provide a valuable resource as they enable reconstruction of participant experience in context. The researcher first needs to develop a high level of trust with the participants. Second, the researcher needs to work with the regularities and routines of the research site and act unobtrusively – like a 'fly on the wall'. While in some research situations the participants quickly overlook the fact that the researcher or camera is observing, in other situations, as a result of researcher or camera presence, the participants may behave in an atypical manner.

Irrespective of the data collection method(s) you plan to use, you will be using the method(s) to source data that will provide an entrée into new understandings. By now you will have figured out the kind of data that will yield the response you expect to get from your research questions. But what about the data that do not provide the kind of response you expect? This data set is too important to ignore. Simply because it challenges your ideal data set does not give you cause to ignore it. It will provide a powerful enriching counter-story and allow you to offer more complete and richer findings than would otherwise be possible.

Data analysis methods

Now you have a clear sense of how you will gather your data. Once the data have been collected they will need to be processed and analysed. The methods that you use to gather and analyse the data are, taken together, known as the research methods. While data gathering is fundamental to an empirical study, the importance of the analysis is not to be understated. It forms the key link between your data and your conclusions. Systematic analytical methods lead to sound results and findings, which then form the basis of the conclusions you draw. Rigorous and appropriate data analytical methods are the goal because they will generate confidence in your findings.

My advice is to resist diving head first into the analysis. Creating a distance between yourself and the data will give you time to consider what emerged during the process of data collecting. That is not to suggest that during this time you should merely be thinking. Now is the time when your interviews, your survey sheets, your field notes, your journals, your video and audio files, your photocopies – and any other precious material that will form your data set – need to be sorted and coded in a way that will be useful to you when you begin your analysis. For example, interviews need to be transcribed. Many doctoral students opt to carry out the transcription themselves, in order to 'get close to the data'. Try to sort and order as much of the data as possible electronically.

Don't be overly concerned if you are beginning to feel overwhelmed by the masses of data you have gathered. It is not uncommon for doctoral students – and for some experienced researchers too – to worry about what sense they might make from the piles of data. Unlike the excitement you felt in the field during the data-gathering phase, the initial analysis stage invariably brings moments of self-doubt. Research is a process full of ups and downs, right from the early planning stages of the project to the final conclusion, as this quote from Gilling indicates:

> The beginning stages in any research project are often intense, busy, plagued by vulnerabilities, endeavours to get things 'right' according to the textbook, or 'experts'' perceptions rather than one's own. Then there is the preparation stage for fieldwork – and a loss of control while waiting, for example, for permission to start; perhaps a delay in getting responses from participants – then the high tension time in the field – and the excitement, the 'wow', the fun, then a drop in the adrenalin stakes when field work is over and the 'hard slog' begins. This is the yo-yo process that is research. (Gilling, 2000, p. 8)

The reason that the analysis stage engenders so much anxiety is simply because there are so many ways of looking at a set of data. One researcher might be intrigued by some aspects of the data, while another will bring another perspective of social reality to the same data set. The sheer complexity of human phenomena allows you to put your unique interpretation on the richness of social life. There is no one right way to interpret data – but, having said that, there are some methods, more than others, that will follow on from your research questions and data collection methods.

Some analytical methods, rather than others, will have a greater fit within your research design. If you took the earlier advice and gave careful consideration to your proposed analysis *before* you collected your data, you will be able to make an early and strong start to the analysis. If, for example, your research involved an historical design, then your analysis might call for a content analysis which examines the content of official documents, diaries, letters, essays, personal notes, media reports and so forth. Or, your design might suggest a Foucauldian analysis that looked more deeply at written texts to explore the relationship between knowledge and forms of power and agency. If your design was ethnographic then you might be interested in discourse analysis to explore how participants use, interpret and reproduce language to convey specific experiences and meanings.

Now that you have had a chance to reflect on the data it is time to organise the data set. It is easier to collate the data before you attempt to make sense of it in relation to the literature. While you were, for example, transcribing interviews and, more generally, creating some semblance of order to your data, you will have had particular thoughts and feelings about the data set. Your reflections and your initial hunches will have identified a number of links and commonalities in your qualitative data and these will form the basis of the patterns you determine are evident in the data. Because this process has the effect of reducing the data set, you need to be prepared to discard some of what might have earlier seemed as crucial to your research. The data reduction process may throw up contradictory data, too, but be sure that you do not discard these uncritically.

You will then be able to code the data by sorting all the different pattern sets into themes that relate in some way to your research questions. Unless your coding framework was pre-specified, it may not be immediately obvious how best to sort the data into themes. A visual approach, such as a concept map, might assist you in moving forward. Alternatively, you might choose to use a software package to help with the organisation of your data into themes or key factors. Of course, any computer program will require direction from you. Thematic clustering, whether assisted electronically or otherwise, is necessarily inferential and interpretive. You need to interpret the data at a surface level and analyse what is said, written and observed. But you should also look beyond the obvious, read between the lines and hear what is unsaid. Exploring the gaps and looking for omissions is a crucial aspect of analysis.

Numerical data also need to be assembled and collated. A number of software packages are available to assist in the statistical analysis of your data and these also provide displays of the data in compact form such as tables, charts, diagrams and graphs. These data displays and analyses are not an end in themselves; the findings they generate require your explanation and interpretation in relation to the context of their production. Keep in mind that voluntary written comments on a questionnaire will not necessarily reflect the views of the entire sample, if only because the participants who feel most strongly one way or another over an issue will be the ones who are more likely to react to the question.

Your discussion around the analysis will require you to account for both typical and atypical responses and to make inferences about the findings in relation to the research questions and to the relevant literature. The task is to create a discussion that does more than state your key themes and findings. What you are aiming for is a synthesis of the data that provides a sense of coherence between each theme. Both confirmatory and contradictory data contribute to a meaningful, credible and plausible discussion which will resonate with what others have already found. Above all, your analysis will demonstrate a scholarly rigour that will generate confidence in your findings.

● Plain sailing?

Now that you have a clear sense of the research design for your study, and have a plan for the way you will collect and analyse the data, you need to be aware that the best-made plans often do not come to fruition. One of the big challenges doctoral students face is in how to deal with unforeseen eventualities. You should consider running a pilot study to check out coverage and procedures on your questionnaire instrument. And you should trial your interview schedule, practise your interviewing skills, and test out your recording equipment with a non-participant. Through the data collection phase, you need to be patient, committed and strong. You need to accommodate your participants' schedules, needs and expectations. Flexibility on your part will go a long way when you are confronted with unanticipated systems reorganisations and personnel changes within your research site. Coping with the ups and downs of the research process is part and parcel of the doctoral journey.

Let's face it: research does not always go according to a plan. Mistakes will be made. There may well be very real difficulties involved in gathering, analysing and managing the data. There will be tedious times, lonely hours, setbacks and scary blocks, particularly during the data collection and analysis phases. Although you might find this difficult to swallow, there will also be people who doubt what you are trying to do and people who have little faith in your ability to undertake this study. There will be others whose 'helpfulness' is not in any way helpful to your work. Along with the privilege of doing research, there is the responsibility – to your participants, to your supervisors, to the discipline – which from time to time might seem overwhelming. However, keep in mind there will also be breakthrough moments when the loneliness, tedium and personal doubts are forgotten in the excitement of new insights.

In the next chapter we bring these ideas together when we work through the development of a research proposal. Whilst there is generally no set format for the proposal, we will look at a number of headings that will guide you towards a suitable proposal structure. We will find that explaining and justifying a proposed study requires thinking, searching, sourcing material, and making firm decisions about a range of aspects that will contribute to your study. It also requires attending to ethical issues in relation to the conduct of the research.

Review

Main points:

- Different research purposes initiate different research designs.
- A well thought-out design provides a coherent plan for undertaking research.
- All research designs are built on theoretical foundations which frame the way the study will be conducted.
- The overall design will allow you to address your research questions.
- Different research designs tend to lend support to specific kinds of data sets.
- Survey, interview and observation are often used to gather social science data.
- Some analytical methods more than others will have a greater fit within your design.
- A scholarly analysis generates confidence in your findings.

Key terms:

- Research design
- Research methodology
- Research methods

Reference

Gilling, M. (ed.) (2000). *Research: The Art of Juggling*. Wellington: Massey University.

5 Getting Underway with the Research Proposal

This chapter looks at:

▶ What is a research proposal?
▶ What needs to be included in a research proposal?
▶ Writing the research proposal
▶ Defending the research proposal
▶ Ethical research

What is a research proposal?

A research proposal is a central feature of the research world and an important step researchers take before they conduct their research. It is a plan for the research that the researcher is hoping to undertake. All researchers write a proposal to clarify what topic is going to be investigated and why it is important, and what processes and procedures will be used; they also address a number of other aspects in relation to the proposed research. Whether the proposed research is to be carried out to meet the requirements for a doctorate, or whether the proposal is written as a bid to secure research funding, the proposal is crucial in that it will both signal the intentions of the researcher to undertake research and outline the way in which the research will be undertaken. It will demonstrate that the researcher is clear about what will be investigated and what it will take to successfully complete the investigation.

The proposal is the formal means by which you step into the apprenticeship of becoming an academic researcher. Up until now, more than likely, you will have been provisionally enrolled as a doctoral student. Your university will require you, within a given time period, to present a case for conducting your research and, typically, the vehicle through which the case is presented is through a written proposal. Invariably, a panel or committee will assess your plan according to its strengths and weaknesses and will provide you with helpful feedback. What the panel will expect to find is sufficient evidence that your proposed study is worth the time and effort you plan to give to it. They want to be sure that the issue you propose to investigate will be worth pursuing and that your plans for addressing the issue are appropriate.

Once the proposal is accepted as a plan for the conduct of research, and once you have obtained ethical clearance, your data collection can take place. In a sense, proposals are written and then subjected to scrutiny to protect both you and the participants involved in your study. The accepted proposal becomes a document that you can refer to in order to inform your work at all stages of the project.

One thing that doctoral researchers quickly learn from writing a research proposal is that, like the literature review, the proposal is a form of research. Explaining and justifying your proposed study to readers and demonstrating its value is an important exercise in your doctoral journey. It will require a clear conceptual framework to put forward a case or argument for your study. It demands thinking, searching, sourcing material and making firm decisions about a range of significant aspects that will contribute to your study. You have already made a number of decisions critical to your study and all these decisions will give you a head start when it comes to developing the proposal.

The thing is that you cannot write a research proposal without first attending to these important research features. That is why our discussion on research proposals is situated after the chapters on literature reviews and methodologies. In the development of your proposal it will be advisable to seek guidance from and support of your intentions from advisers. Once firm decisions have been made, the task of writing the proposal becomes very manageable. In fact, many doctoral students look back on this stage as the first time that everything about the project began to come together.

What needs to be included in a research proposal?

The proposal provides a basic outline of your entire research. Irrespective of topic area and discipline, your research proposal will read like an essay that offers an overview of your intended research. In the proposal you develop an argument or make a case for your intended research. The purpose of making a case in the proposal is to convince the approval panel that you know what you are doing, that you can establish why it is worth doing, and that you have thought through issues in relation to the conduct (and implications) of what you plan to do. So that readers can make sense of the argument you put forward, you will need to write the proposal in plain English. A well-written proposal clarifies your plans and insights in a way that allows readers to follow the development from research problem to research answer. It helps readers understand the researcher's intentions and how the findings will contribute to knowledge.

Some universities require you to submit your proposal on an official template with predetermined headings. Others leave the format to you.

However, if the format is of your choosing, there will still be an expectation that you identify what issue your proposed research will investigate, how you will go about addressing the issue, what we will learn from the study, and why you consider it is important to carry out. A word limit for the proposal will often be imposed. Regulations at some universities require you to defend your proposal orally at a specifically convened meeting. Most universities will require your proposal to be endorsed by your supervisors. Bear in mind, however, that gaining supervisors' approval does not absolve you of full responsibility for the proposal submitted.

Activity

Check out the requirements that must be satisfied at your university for doctoral research proposals.

1. When will the proposal need to be submitted?
2. Is there a template or standard form to be used?
3. What is the word limit for the proposal?
4. Are specific headings required?
5. Are supervisors' signatures required to endorse the proposal?
6. Is there a requirement to defend the proposal?

The point to keep in mind is that the requirements set by your university must be adhered to. If you can follow the proposal guidelines, then, often, the assumption is that you can probably follow through on what you propose to do in your study. This could well be your first big test in the research stakes. Be sure, first, that you know what is expected of you, and second, that you do not deviate from the requirements.

Your proposal will need a clear organisational structure so that a panel of non-experts can understand what is planned. That means it should be written in a user-friendly way. It will need a table of contents that lists the sections in the order they appear in the proposal and the page number on which each section can be found. The proposal should be organised in such a way that you are able to clarify the aim of the research, justify its undertaking, set it within the context of relevant literature, outline your research data collection and analysis methods and who will participate, describe the resources needed and the time frame, and outline the contribution to knowledge that the project will make.

Checklist of possible sections for research proposals
1. Title
2. Abstract
3. Introduction
4. Research questions
5. Conceptual framework and theory
6. Literature review
7. Methodology
8. Significance
9. Limitations
10. Ethical issues
11. References
12. Appendices (e.g., timetable, budget, protocols, etc.)

These are the headings that are often used in research proposals. However, researchers do not always work on the proposal sections in the order that is finally presented in written form. The introduction is a case in point. It provides a summary of background information, definitions, context, summary of past research, and a rationale for the study. Many researchers choose to clarify their thinking by first working on subsequent sections, and hence the introduction is often one of the last sections completed. While you are working on one part of the subsequent sections it is likely that other parts will change or be refined so that various 'parts' of the proposal are overlapping, so as to speak, in your mind simultaneously. Your final proposal might look as though it has been developed through a logical progression because it has an integrity that is sound, but in all probability, you will develop it sporadically.

Proposals need a clear statement of purpose and a well-planned literature review which typically begins with the broad topic and gradually narrows the focus. Moreover, proposals need a research question(s) and possibly sub-questions, a research design, a proposed analytical framework, and a discussion on limitations and ethics in relation to the conduct of the study. Let us look at these components and their function in more detail.

The title

The title gives the reader a clear sense of what you are investigating. The words you choose in your title should encapsulate succinctly, and in a compelling manner, what you plan to do.

The abstract

An abstract is often provided as a summary of the key features of the research. It is often restricted to around 100 words and will identify the topic, purpose, theory, methodology and significance of the study, as well as the argument underwriting the research. You can get a sense of what will follow from reading abstracts of successful proposals or articles in high-ranking journals within your discipline.

The introduction

The introduction lets the reader know something about the topic and what has already been discovered about it, and why you are interested in pursuing it further. You will need to try and engage the reader from the start by building a rationale for your study and situating it within a social and historical context. You might want to locate yourself within the study by clarifying your personal background and knowledge in relation to this study. You then lead into a clear statement of the purpose of the study: what your overall aim is and what objectives you expect to achieve. And importantly, you tell the reader why this research is important, why it needs to be undertaken, what contribution it will make to the field of knowledge and, in broad terms, what the wider implications might be.

The research questions

You need to be clear exactly what your central guiding research questions are. These will identify the overall focus of the study and, hence, follow on naturally from the statement of purpose. Sub-questions break the central questions down into manageable parts to be addressed directly in the study. Many students confuse the sub-questions with the questions that are developed for questionnaire purposes. Be sure that non-trivial answers can be found to the research questions.

If your study is of a quantitative design, such as a causal-comparative or correlational study, you will provide a statement of your research hypothesis.

The conceptual framework and theory

Any study needs organisation and you need to show that you have thought about this by clarifying how you will approach the issue under question. For example, you might list the themes or issues that you will be investigating in a qualitative study, or you might provide a diagram or chart, or perhaps an historical study might be organised by time periods. At this point you might want to make explicit the key terms and expressions or variables that are used in your study and clarify to readers the particular definitions of these terms that will be drawn upon.

Your study is likely to be anchored within a theoretical framework and underpinned by particular philosophical assumptions. The theory or theories you find appropriate to the kind of work you plan need to be discussed and their use in your study justified. If your study is focused more on theory development, then you need to clarify that theory generation will be the role played by theory in your study.

The literature review

The literature review serves an important function and is usually fairly extensive. It reports on what is known in your area by focusing on what has been done before, and is intended to highlight major shortfalls or a 'gap' in the current knowledge base. In that sense it provides a context for your own study. The review will establish why it is deemed necessary to conduct the proposed research and what your study will contribute to the conversation.

In the literature review you will do more than summarise published articles, records and documents in the area. In addition to mapping out the field, you will need to synthesise the literature base and offer a critique. As well, do not assume that readers can readily see the connections between the literature and your own study: make clear links for them. The review you provide in the research proposal is not expected to be your final draft for your thesis. Since you will be constantly engaging with the literature in the area as your study proceeds, your review may well change to accommodate new ideas and report on new findings.

You should be aware that, as a doctoral student, there are three literature bases with which you will need to be familiar: the theoretical literature (noted above under 'Conceptual framework and theory'), the substantive literature (usually referred to as the 'Literature review') and the methodological literature (noted below under 'Methodology').

The methodology

The methodology section discusses in detail how you will collect, analyse and present the data from the research. The choice of methods should be appropriate to the research questions. This section will clarify the research design and establish whether the study is, for example, ethnographic, action research, case study, or another design. It will describe what tools you will use to gather data and who will take part in the study. It will discuss the methodological literature in relation to your research focus and the criteria you employed to make your methodological decisions. Your discussion will provide a justification that your methods are feasible and appropriate to answer your research question.

In this section you need to be extremely clear about what is going to happen in your study. Be explicit about where your study will take place, when it is going to happen, and how you will gain access to the site. Describe who is going to be involved, as well as why and how you will select those people. You also need to tell the reader by what means you are going to gather the data. Will you interview, observe, survey, test, gather documentation, photograph, or will you collect your data by other means? Will you use a questionnaire or interview schedule? If so, what themes, issues and broad questions are you intending to explore? Are you able to provide your research protocols in relation to the questionnaire or the interview schedule? Are you planning to audiotape or videotape your participants? How are you intending to organise, display and analyse all the data that you collect? Have you addressed issues of validity and reliability in relation to your study?

The significance

You will have some idea, based on previous research, of the sorts of outcomes you expect from your study. Your proposal needs to say why these outcomes might be significant to, for example, policy, the profession, and the discipline. You will want to outline how your study advances knowledge and extends understandings provided in the literature of the area under investigation. Doctoral students sometimes exaggerate the importance of their proposed study. Remember that you will be making a small contribution to knowledge, rather than one that is earth shattering.

The limitations

Any research finding is limited to the study at hand and researchers are mindful of these limitations. It is best to be frank about this and discuss the ways in which your design and the specific conditions within it may create limitations. You might want to discuss how your sample, the specific research site, the particular questions you are intending to ask, your limited access to documents and so forth are likely to impose constraints on the study. You need to show that you know your findings cannot speak for everyone, in every context and for every time, but that they will still have credibility.

Ethical issues

Your university's code of ethical conduct for research involving human subjects will guide your study. You must be able to assure the reader that you understand the importance of ethical behaviour in the production of knowledge and that you have addressed issues related to the participants in your study. In particular, you will need to demonstrate your responsibility to protect the confidentiality, anonymity and the physical and mental well-being of the participants in your research.

The references

Your proposal should identify only the texts cited, and should reflect both 'search' and 'research' in the style preferred by your discipline. A good reference list is invaluable.

The appendices (e.g., budget, instruments, etc.)

Estimate, if necessary, the financial costs involved in your study with a detailed budget. Whilst budgets are not always required of doctoral students in the proposal, it is understood that you will give some consideration to this aspect. Include any research protocols: for example, the participants' information letter and consent form, a questionnaire, or the planned interview questions. Each new protocol is labelled as a new appendix and needs to be noted in the body of the proposal.

Included in the appendices should be a timeline for the study, listing the times and dates for each step of your research process. A timeline demonstrates that you have given serious consideration to how you are going manage all the activities involved in the research process. In Chapter 1 we looked at an anticipated timeline for doctoral study. Now is the time to create your own timeline. You might want to refer back to Chapter 1 for guidance. As you journey through your doctorate, the timeline will serve as a reminder of the phases you have accomplished and what needs to be done next. In the early stages, particularly, focus on the immediate and avoid being overwhelmed by the many tasks listed on your timetable. As you enter each new milestone phase you might find the need to write yourself a finer-grained timetable for that phase. Print off your broad overview timetable and pin it onto a noticeboard where it will be in easy view.

Activity

- Construct a timeline that accounts for the important phases in your research process.
- List the key phases of your research and the period of time that you are able to allocate to each of those phases.

● Writing the research proposal

Planning organiser

Key aspects	Key aspects related to my study
Main objective	
Research questions	
Important literature	
Theoretical framework	
Research design	
Data collection	
Data analysis methods	

In order to get you prepared for writing your proposal, copy the table above, allowing for more space where needed to complete entries in the form of notes. If you have worked through Chapters 1 to 4 in this book, you will have already given considerable thought to these key elements related to your study. You will have made decisions on your topic and formulated your research questions. You will have made a good start on your literature review and you will have framed the design of your study. You will know who you want to be involved as participants in your study and will know by what means you will access and analyse your data.

The next stage is to transform these notes into a discussion. We will begin with a written discussion of at most two pages. Set aside one page for what your research is trying to find out and for setting out the background, and allow one page for how you plan to carry out your research. Writing a couple of pages will help you identify the important aspects of your study that you need to convey to others. In addition, you might want to talk to a friend or partner (particularly someone unfamiliar with your topic area) about your proposed research. What is particularly helpful about both these approaches is that they force you to confront precisely what, why and how you plan to do your research.

Notice that your written discussion is easily divided into two sections: (i) the introductory information and (ii) the research design. This is a guide for your proposal. The first half of the proposal will report on the first stages of the research. It will provide a description of the topic under investigation, offer a synthesis and analysis of past research relevant to the topic, and establish a need for the study by noting the gaps in earlier work in the area. It is written in the present and past tense. The second half of the proposal will focus specifically on what you plan to do and will outline how you plan to do it. It will describe what information needs to be gathered, how it will be obtained and from whom, and will identify the theoretical framework that will serve as an explanatory resource for the study. It will be written in the future tense.

Both sections together provide a broad picture of the proposed study. Although the proposal sets out a plan for what you intend to research, as well as how, why and when you will research it, you should consider it as a working document. You may well refine certain aspects as the research proceeds. A degree of flexibility is built into the plan to accommodate changes in the context and setting of the study and for you to make adjustments when things go wrong. Just as plans for new buildings are sometimes varied as a result of, say, the availability of materials, so too are research plans open to change in response to, say, the availability of resources and participants. Of course, you will only be making changes when you have discussed all options with your supervisor and when modifications are deemed absolutely necessary. At all costs, avoid wasting your precious doctoral time on unnecessary change.

Now that you have written two pages and possibly talked to others about your proposed research, you need to expand on your written material and spoken ideas to develop a convincing case for your plan. Using the headings described above will make it easier. Subheadings might also be used to lend support to further detail within a heading. You should adopt a style that is not overly formal but one that creates an engaging discussion. If possible, check the style in which recent successful proposals in your discipline have been written and identify a style with which you feel comfortable.

The thing to know is that proposal writing takes time. In fact it will probably take you through more drafts than you anticipated. Allow more time than you think will be necessary so that the final document will be completed in good time. Ultimately, you will want your proposal to be assessed as well constructed, well argued and reasoned, and factually correct. You want it to demonstrate a logical consistency between its various elements so that you can convey to others that you have the argumentative and analytical skills required to make a contribution to knowledge.

Careless, loose and apologetic writing and unnecessary jargon will not do you any favours and is likely to label you as a risk in the doctoral stakes. Remember to conform to citation and referencing conventions. Since your readers may not be totally familiar with your field of study your proposal needs to be, simultaneously, clear and concise, and fully comprehensible to and sufficiently comprehensive for all readers. As you are nearing completion of the final draft, ask yourself if you feel that you know exactly what the proposed research is about, how it will be conducted, what will we all learn from it, and why it is worth doing. In your view, has any information been omitted that, if included, would make this proposal stronger? Is any information redundant?

● Defending the research proposal

In addition to a written proposal your university may require you to defend your proposal orally to the approval panel or admissions board. If the proposal is made clear and justifiable to the satisfaction of the panel or admissions board, you will be fully registered within the doctoral programme. Since oral defence meetings are often formal occasions, you will need to be confident that you can explain and justify your plan and answer the panel's questions in order to convince the panel of the merits of the proposed research. Don't assume that the audience knows as much about the topic as you do. Equally, however, remember that the audience is an academic one, so pitch your presentation appropriately. In particular, you need to convince the panel that:

- the scope, quality and methods of the research you propose are likely to warrant the award of a doctorate
- the research as proposed is viable in terms of the word and time limits required of a doctoral thesis.

In addition, the panel will assess whether or not you will receive adequate supervision and will have access to the material resources required to conduct your research. The meeting will not only give you an opportunity to present information to an audience of varying expertise, experience and knowledge, but, perhaps more importantly, it will also allow you to receive feedback on your proposed work. On the one hand, you may receive a positive endorsement for the way you plan to conduct the research before the research gets underway. On the other hand, the panel's differing viewpoints may alert you to aspects that you had overlooked. Use this feedback to your advantage to enhance your proposed study.

Some students feel threatened about this particular milestone which requires them to speak with some authority about their planned research;

others seem to relish the opportunity. If you are one of the former then here are a few suggestions:

- be thoroughly prepared and try to anticipate the questions asked
- be positive and enthusiastic about what you are planning to research
- know your audience
- talk confidently and slowly
- use eye contact
- use pauses
- use technology, and visual and print aids purposefully
- conclude confidently
- practise before the event.

Liaise with your supervisor about the kinds of questions that the audience might ask you. When it is time to deal with the questions, listen carefully. If you do not understand the question, ask the questioner to repeat it. If you still do not know the answer, then say so. Be honest, rather than pretend to know. The important thing to remember about the defence of your research proposal is that you have to make a case for the study. You need to persuade the panel that this research needs to proceed. But don't try to impress with difficult terms and expressions. Keep it simple and above all, provide your audience with clarity. Perhaps the best advice is that you make an effort to attend proposal defences of other students in your discipline at your university so that you can get a sense of what is expected of you and what the procedures are.

● Ethical research

Ethical research involves decision making during all aspects of the process. From the project's very inception right through to the reporting of the project in the written thesis and in journals and other media, the point is that you will need to make decisions that are ethical. Decision making never takes place in isolation and will always have particular effects. Ethical decision making responds to the question 'What is the morally right course of action to take?' in a way that meets appropriate standards and ethical norms focused on best outcomes for human beings. As researcher, you will have ultimate control, power and influence over the ways in which you proceed and the kinds of outcomes that are produced; because of that, it is of fundamental importance that your decisions at all stages in your doctoral research journey are ethically informed. You need to be able to justify that all your decisions demonstrate ethical behaviour and integrity on your part.

Research integrity

Research integrity is one of the major ethical considerations. To demonstrate research integrity requires you to demonstrate your commitment to the pursuit of knowledge in your discipline and your commitment to undertaking and reporting on the research in an honest manner. In the first instance, your research will need to meet doctoral standards of adequacy. It must demonstrate that you have carefully thought through all aspects of the process. Importantly, your project must have clear research goals and the design you plan must make it possible for these goals to be met. The research needs to be justified on the basis of a need or a gap observed from a comprehensive and critical yet balanced examination of existing literature.

Your research plan will provide a clear outline of the boundaries of the project and of the assumptions on which the scope of the study has been developed. It will offer a description of the methodology and research methods that you have chosen, justified on the grounds of unsuitability of alternative approaches as assessed from the methodological literature. If an innovative methodology is chosen, you will need to demonstrate the validity of the approach and show that your design complies with the standards set by professional peers. You will need to be clear on the basis on which your participants will be selected and ensure that they have not been chosen to achieve a particular research objective or outcome that you have in mind.

In order to undertake the doctoral research that you propose, you will need to address the issue of your own competence to carry out the work. You will require obvious skills, experience and expertise. If you do not have these currently, you will need to be clear that such competencies will be gained in a way that will not compromise the research timeline. Discuss these competency issues, along with all other ethical concerns associated with the research, with your supervisor.

As the researcher, you are the person who will be controlling the way in which knowledge is produced in the research. Since you will be controlling how data are collected, interpreted and selected for analysis, you need to comply with the ethical standards for data collection, analysis and reporting that have been developed within your discipline. You must ensure that you avoid influencing the responses of your participants, that you do not falsify or purposely exclude or destroy data, and that you check any statistical calculations. Be sure that you attribute, with proper citation, any data, words or ideas of another person. All data and information must be reported with utmost integrity to avoid the presentation of an inaccurate presentation of the findings.

New researchers sometimes feel concerned that the data gathered are not what they expected – but, at all costs, avoid manipulating the data in any way in order to present more desirable findings. Providing incomplete, inaccurate and unchecked data may be looked upon as practices involving deception. To safeguard your practices, you might consider keeping a record of the decisions you made, and the reasons for those decisions, in relation to the collection and analysis of your data set. You should write up the methodological decisions in your thesis in a way that makes it abundantly clear how the data collection and analysis process proceeded. Such detail will allow readers to make connections between your findings and the methods employed to achieve them.

It is important to recognise that data are not owned by the researcher but rather are in the researcher's (and supervisor's) safe keeping. You are responsible for looking after them. You need to safeguard confidential information. In fact, you need to ensure that all your data from the research are stored in a secure repository for a given period of time beyond the research to enable subsequent analysis or possible challenge to your findings. After the given time frame the data will be destroyed. You need to ensure that the location in which the research is stored must not be accessible to anyone other than those associated with the research. Access to the stored data should be negotiated with participants.

Respect for persons

In addition to research integrity, the other major ethical consideration for your project is respect for persons. The considerations of justice and benevolence follow on from these. Respect for persons involves the recognition of the dignity, beliefs and privacy of people. It requires treating people as autonomous agents and protecting their rights. Respect for persons also implies that people with diminished autonomy or competence and those identified as vulnerable are entitled to additional protection.

One way to begin your ethical decision making, in relation to respect for persons, is to reflect on who and what might be affected, both directly and indirectly, by your research. Think in terms of individuals, communities, present and future society, and so on. Once identified, you will be in a stronger position to ensure that you take the necessary steps to protect their rights. Rights protection is, of course, fundamental to the collection of authentic and valid data. Your decision making will ensure that you will demonstrate benevolence towards each person affected by your research and that you will treat each in a just and fair manner. You will ensure that each is protected from harm, that benefits are maximised, and that your practices will be principled on notions of justice.

How do these ethical considerations become operationalised in your research process? They require that your decisions surrounding the recruitment of participants are made equitably and on the grounds of their relationship to your research questions. Once participants have been selected you need to provide them with full details of the research so that they are able to provide free (and not coerced) consent with regard to the information provided. Informed consent must be obtained for all participants, and those participants who are classified as minors will need consent from a parent or guardian. Be aware that informed consent does not mean that consent automatically continues throughout the study. It means that participants have the right to voluntarily withdraw their participation during any part of the study and do not need to provide reasons for their withdrawal. You will need to respect this right.

Be mindful that the language you use must be easily comprehensible to your participants. It means that you should avoid academic language. It requires you to write about the purpose of the study, who is conducting it and their contact details, what is required of their involvement and whether consent may need to be renegotiated. It requires you to spell out, in language your participants will understand, what the benefits and the potential risks or harm (e.g., physical, psychological, emotional or exploitative), if any, are likely to be. If you have identified likely harm to your participants, you need to consider seriously whether new research questions and a new research design might be called for, since exposure to unnecessary harm is not deemed ethical.

As an ethical researcher, your respect for persons entails more than transparency of purpose, of participation, of benefits and of potential harm. It involves developing a research culture in which trust and confidentiality prevail. There are particular issues that need attending to when researching other cultures.

Case study

Kylie is a New Zealand-born Samoan. She wants to research young Pasifika people in schooling. Her Master's thesis investigated the conflicts young Pasifika people face between the expectations demanded of them by their culture and those expectations within New Zealand's educational system. As a result of her Master's findings, her local community became more aware of the differences in the assumptions and practices within the two cultures. She hopes to build on this study in her doctoral work and provide deeper insights for the local community.   ➤

Kylie is very aware of the relatively poor academic performance of Pasifika secondary school students. Her local community is very keen to find out exactly what it is that happens to their young people, and, because of their support and advice, she has decided to formalise their assistance by establishing a Pasifika elders advisory group. Since she wants to listen to the stories of young people, she is also thinking that a Pasifika youth advisory group might be useful.

Working in two cultures means that she will need to develop a research methodology that is able to deal with cross-cultural differences. Although at this stage she is not sure whether she will also observe in classrooms, whether or not she will talk with teachers, or whether she will focus only on the students' stories, she wonders what the effects of being a New Zealand-born Samoan – an 'insider' – might mean for the research.

Researchers working in any environment need to be sure that they do not violate the rights of informed consent. As a researcher you must ensure that your processes and practices are those that are agreed to by your participants. Participants have the right to see the data you have collected on them personally and, typically, you will provide them, for editing purposes, with the transcripts of your interviews with them. Your private research notes are your domain, however, and need not be disclosed.

As researcher, you must take all necessary steps to keep all information and records safe and to protect the privacy and confidentiality of participants. Since confidentiality can never be absolutely guaranteed, you need to make this point clear to participants. It is your responsibility to ensure anonymity by removing all identifying material of the research site and of the participants. You need to take particular care that participants are not identifiable from data sources created from audio or video recordings. If anonymity is not possible, or if the research participants request that they be named in the final report, then you will need to negotiate their request formally.

Ethics applications

The principles of research integrity and respect for persons during the undertaking of research will have been codified within your university. Codes of ethical and professional conduct for research have been developed by a number of different disciplines including psychology (e.g., the American Psychological Association, APA; the British Psychological Society, BPS), sociology (e.g., the British Sociological Association, BSA), education (e.g., the American Educational Research Association, AERA; the British Educational Research Association, BERA), and anthropology (e.g., the American

Anthropological Association, AAA). These professional ethical standards have been developed and adopted from an understanding of the rights and responsibilities of human beings in relation to the specific research undertaken within the discipline. The standards will also be informed by the 1949 Nuremberg Code, based on the principles of voluntary consent, the avoidance of harm, social good, and ongoing risk analysis, and constructed around the point that it is indefensible to treat human beings as objects and as a means to the researcher's ends.

Codes of ethical practice at your university

Your university will have its own formalised code of ethical practice for the conduct of research involving human participants and your research must comply with this code. The intention of the code is to provide protection to you and your research participants, as well as the university. More than likely you will be required to submit an application to the committee responsible for ethical research for assurance that you have undertaken an ethical analysis of your proposed project and that all ethical issues have been dealt with adequately. Some universities have streamlined the application process for 'low risk' research. Whether deemed 'low risk' or not, your proposed research will need ethical clearance before you recruit your participants and begin data collection.

Activity

Search the website of your institution and locate its code of ethical conduct for research with human participants.

1. Read the regulations and procedures carefully.
2. List the ethical concerns that accompany your project.
3. Consider the measures that could be put in place to ensure the ethical integrity of your project.
4. Download an application form from your institution's site.
5. Complete a first draft of the application form.

You will have noticed that completing the ethics application is a time-consuming process. It is quite likely that your first draft will not necessarily represent your final application. In fact, some committees may want to interview you or, at the very least, ask you to reflect again on the ethical implications of your application. If you have not allowed sufficient time for ethical clearance in the timetable you developed earlier in this chapter then you will need to make some amendments.

"The most frustrating part of it was trying to get through the human ethics jungle. It took a long time for me because I had to do a full application and had to work through that with my supervisor to her satisfaction. There was a lot of toing and froing, to the point where I thought we had gone around in circles so much that I submitted something to the human ethics committee because I thought that that was the only way we were going to move forward."

The application focuses primarily on the link between your research methods and your participants. While you will need to explain the purpose of the research, the committee will be looking carefully at your plan for recruiting participants and for accessing the research site as well as your expectations of and proposed interactions with participants in the study. You will also likely be asked for any letters of information, consent forms, transcribers' agreements, all of which will provide a measure for the particular way you will deal with the needs and rights of participants and with the integrity of the project. Once approval has been received you will be able to begin the truly exciting component of the research – the work 'in the field'.

In the next chapter we will explore a range of support that is available to you during the doctoral journey. We will look at how that support will help turn your study into an enriching experience. Your supervisor will be the primary means of support during the doctoral journey. We will look at the importance of developing shared understandings with your supervisors in relation to how the supervision arrangement will work.

Review

Main points:

- A research proposal is a central feature of all research activity.
- Proposals describe the intentions of the researcher and outline how the research will be undertaken.
- A proposal cannot be written without serious attention to the literature and methodological issues relevant to your research questions.
- The proposal clarifies and justifies the aims, contextualised within the literature. It outlines the research methods, describing who will participate and the resources needed, and it provides a timeline.

- Some universities require that the proposal be defended orally.
- All research must comply with codes of ethical practice.
- Ethics applications address issues to do with research integrity and respect for persons.

Key terms:

- Research proposal
- Defence of the proposal
- Ethical practice

6 Getting Alongside Support

This chapter looks at:

▶ Support from the university
▶ Support from the library
▶ Support from peers and colleagues
▶ Supervisor selection
▶ Roles and responsibilities around supervision
▶ Making the supervision arrangement work
▶ Resolving supervision issues

● Support from the university

Your doctoral study is a shared responsibility. The university, at the overarching level, provides frameworks, policies, regulations and codes of conduct that set you up for success in your doctoral programme. Within those management structures lie a range of units, such as graduate research schools, and departments, as well as a number of individuals, such as deans and supervisors, all of whom will be responsible for establishing processes and creating arrangements that contribute to your success. You, of course, are the central player in this arrangement. Getting alongside the armoury of support at your disposal requires certain responsibilities from you, just as it provides you with certain rights.

Your university will be very keen for you to succeed. Not only does the university want you to succeed for your own personal benefit, it will also want you to succeed for the financial rewards your timely completion will bring to the university. It is little wonder, then, that the university will do its utmost to enhance your doctoral experience. It will ensure that efficient systems are in place to provide you with the infrastructural support you need and the human and material resources necessary for you to complete your thesis. Thesis supervision, library, English language support, seminars, workshops, online materials, handbooks, induction programmes, technological support, doctoral funding, and doctoral student representation on doctoral committees are just some of the ways in which your university will be supporting your doctoral journey.

A system designed to help you succeed needs to build in accountability measures. At regular intervals your progress will be monitored, which, for you, will mean paperwork involving the completion of forms. Typically, in the pro forma, you set a number of targets for the next monitoring period and, as well, outline the ways in which you have met the objectives you set out for the past time frame. Your supervisor will provide a short report on your progress. While you may feel some resentment towards the progress report requirement, and may perhaps view it as an unwelcome interference with the thesis work, in effect the reports do serve the purpose of recording your work over a period of time. Students often find the records useful for looking back on their personal growth and intellectual development.

● **Support from the library**

Your programme of study will provide you with access to the library at your institution as soon as your enrolment is confirmed. The library is your most important resource, besides your supervisor, for the successful completion of your study. Early on in your study you will have had a one-on-one consultation (either face to face or otherwise) with the librarian responsible for your discipline at your university and will have discovered what assistance the library offers.

The library will provide you with access to recent literature in your chosen field of study. Databases that host a wide range of publications allow you to search widely for relevant literature. In addition, within your specific discipline, the library will provide guides to selected information resources such reference resources and websites. More importantly, perhaps, the library will offer you access to electronic and/or paper copies of the most recent articles from a range of journals, as well as access to many of the latest books, periodicals and reports relevant to your work.

Libraries often provide an inter-library loan service for a small fee, and will usually inter-loan books and journal articles. Typically, libraries will also offer a mechanism for you to set up journal alerts, which will make it possible for you to receive details of the latest issues of your chosen journals. Libraries value doctoral students' recommendations for the purchase of research-related materials ranging from books to DVDs. They also invariably provide an online research tool on their site to assist researchers with information and advice relating to aspects such as qualitative and quantitative research, research design, writing and literature reviews.

● **Support from peers and colleagues**

Your personal growth and intellectual development is enhanced by the research culture at your university. Such development is available to you through means of intangible support as a consequence of your membership of the research community within your department. There is a lot to be said about being around other similarly minded people. Use their enthusiasm about new insights within the field and their methods of solving intellectual problems as a way of learning tacitly about the way in which academics think and act. Use it as support for the work you are doing. Use it as an incentive for completing the next piece of thesis work.

> *"I was around a lot of experienced researchers and they got to know me. I think it's important to come into social spaces like the common room; you strike up conversations with people and they inevitably ask you what you are doing. So you try and explain and in the explaining you tend to clarify your own thoughts about things. But you also often get some really good suggestions from people about things to consider."*

Then there are doctoral student peers. They will not necessarily be able to offer sound advice on writing and illuminating discussions on thesis direction but they will provide a valuable means of support and a listening ear.

> *"I've made connections with some of the other doctoral students here on campus. Because I'm further down the process than they are, it's been an opportunity for us to just talk about my experience and how it compares to theirs and what they can expect in the future."*

Affirmation of what you are doing is important at all stages of the process, even when you are proceeding confidently. Emotional support is particularly important when the burden of undertaking the thesis weighs heavily on your shoulders: times when the writing is not progressing, when there are difficulties accessing the research site or participants, when the data do not seem to be supporting your hunches, and, in short, when any kind of problem blocks your way forward. Being accountable to a peer or a colleague on a regular basis may be all you need to assist you in navigating your way through the block.

> *"Probably the biggest personal skill was recognising that – it's not really a skill – but recognition that I would not be able to do this without making a commitment to someone else each week. So I've found it invaluable having a weekly meeting with my colleague. That's made a huge difference for both of us because I think when you are a distance student it can be quite isolating."*

Support of a more academic nature, beyond that received from within your immediate research community, is available if you network. Online or face-to-face doctoral cohort discussion or seminar groups organised within your discipline often provide the intellectual support needed to review or test out your ideas or direction, to solve an issue, or to add breadth to your literature base. Conference attendance – and especially conference paper presentations – are guaranteed to develop your skills and generate interest in your work. For one thing, if your conference paper is published, your work becomes known and accessible to a far-reaching readership and becomes the kernel of discussion within a larger networking group. You might, for example, choose to develop your literature review, or write about your innovative methodology. If you present your paper at the conference, your audience might well provide the encouragement in your work that you are desperately seeking. Then again, the audience might offer counter-arguments, questioning your approach and challenging you to think differently. Members of the audience might offer points of theoretical difference, valuable references related to your work, as well as creative solutions to a specific problem. All these audience responses to your presentation will help move your thesis along.

> **"**I went to a couple of conferences. Both had organised a workshop day for doctoral students before the conference and so you got to meet doctoral students all over the world – people studying in the same field – which was just brilliant. Because suddenly there was a room full of people who understood the language that I was talking and, you know, who could relate to the theory, or different theories, and you could see how they had applied them in their own way.**"**

● Supervisor selection

The most influential form of support you receive during your doctoral study will almost certainly be provided by your supervisor (sometimes referred to as 'tutor' or 'thesis adviser'). Your supervisor is the principal resource for your study, and because of that, getting a good match is extremely important. You may not have any say in the matter, in which case you will find yourself assigned a staff member who will be responsible for guiding you through your doctoral study. Of course, that is not to suggest that the supervisor has given consent to the arrangement without full knowledge of what lies in store. Indeed, if you are progressing directly to doctoral study from honours or Master's level, there is a very good chance that your credentials as an independent thinker and committed worker, who will in all likelihood complete on time and without undue coaching, will be well known and will have factored heavily in the supervisor's decision making. In that decision making, your compatibility with the supervisor's personal style will also likely be taken into account.

On the other hand, you may find yourself in the position of nominating your own supervisor. It is not an especially onerous task if you have had the opportunity to work with a potential supervisor before. You will already know which staff members you work well with. However, choice of supervisor can become an unenviable responsibility if your earlier study was not undertaken at the university where your doctoral study will take place. Beyond an online search of departmental staff, looking at their experience, research interests and publications, you will not necessarily know the particular staff, least of all know how you might interrelate. In that case, it will be fundamentally important to start asking knowledgeable others about a potential supervisor. Find out what doctoral experience the supervisor has as well as the reputation and track record that goes hand in hand with that experience. In brief, assess the potential that the supervisor will bring to the supervision before you commit.

Supervisor selection is fundamentally important precisely because you will work with this individual for the next few years. You require a relationship that is effective and productive for you both to ensure that the thesis is completed on time, and, importantly, to ensure that you grow intellectually. An effective supervision relationship, like any relationship, demands considerable effort and goodwill from both parties. It is a complex relationship because, on the one hand, you certainly do not want to be told what to do every step of the way. Rather, you want to be able to take charge of the doctorate. Yet, on the other hand, nor do you want to be left to your own devices. You want balanced support that consists of sufficient care and attention to progress the project and to develop the skills and knowledge that will contribute to you becoming a professional researcher.

Many doctoral students have two supervisors, one of whom will assume primary responsibility for the supervision and the coordination of activities. Ideally, the supervisors will have complementary expertise that, taken together, will guide and inform the academic direction of your work. A supervision team or panel is sometimes formed to contribute a range of specialist knowledges and expertise to the project. A team bringing in multiple perspectives and the possibility of multiple networks is not to be underestimated. However, since specialist knowledges and expertise of supervisors are occasionally grounded in different world views, care needs to be taken that your supervision team members are not likely to provide you with conflicting advice or approaches. Be sure to check this out before you commit to the team assigned. You want everyone 'on the same wavelength' and working towards the same goal.

Maria's doctoral study was based within the anthropology department at her university. She planned an ethnographic study in a school and wanted to explore senior school students' personal meaning making of ethnic identity. She hoped to contextualise her in-depth study of a small group of students with a large survey of similar-aged students' understandings of ethnic identity. She thought it would be important that her supervisors had expertise in anthropology, in sociology, in education, in survey design and in ethnography. To that end, her supervision consisted of a team of three who, together, had the requisite skills and knowledge to advise and guide her through her doctoral work. The three supervisors established their respective roles and agreed on the division of areas of responsibilities early on in the supervision. The supervisor with expertise in anthropology took on the role of principal supervisor. The other supervisors took on lesser responsibilities, offering guidance on the project in relation to their specific knowledge and skill base. Since all three supervisors got on well together and had the student's doctoral project's interests at heart, the supervision meetings were collegial and friendly. Maria, for her part, engaged in the cross-disciplinary exchange of ideas without having to compromise her world view.

● Roles and responsibilities around supervision

When supervisors give their approval to oversee your project, what they are doing is expressing confidence in your project. They are implicitly expressing the view that your project is promising, that it is likely to contribute to knowledge, and that it is manageable within the given time frame. They may be basing their assessment on their first-time reading of your research proposal or, simply, on your explanations to them of your intentions. Alternatively, they may well have assisted you with direction and feedback on your proposal and, in that case, will be very familiar with the details of your proposed research design and your proposed data collection and analysis.

In agreeing to supervise your project, supervisors need to juggle a number of roles and responsibilities, ranging from the administration aspects of the project to the enhancement of your intellectual growth. They will ensure that you are familiar with all the relevant policies, regulations and codes of conduct and will draw your attention to specific rulings. They will make you aware of any financial assistance available and will offer guidance when you apply for internal and external funding for your project. They will be sure that you complete all the requisite forms and progress reports of your work and that you complete them in a timely manner. They will take care that you fully understand any ethical, safety or legal concerns relating to the project and assist you with relevant applications.

In order to enhance your doctoral learning, they will want to draw your attention to the resources available and to any workshops, seminars, conferences and technological or statistical support on offer. They will want to guide you in your planning and in the execution of the project, contributing ideas in relation to the literature, to the theoretical grounding and to the research methods. Because they believe that the project carries much promise, they will want to engage you in scholarly conversation surrounding the ideas in your work.

Your project completion is the overriding goal for the supervisor. Not only must your supervisor establish support structures and enable interactions that are conducive to timely completion of the project and that contribute to an enriching experience for you, but he or she must ensure that standards are upheld to the satisfaction of doctoral stakeholders from the institution and the discipline. In order to carry out the multi-dimensional role, your supervisor provides an ethic of care that sits alongside an ethos of confidence in your capabilities, bringing to the arrangement a vast array of competencies: research expertise; an awareness of and compliance with expected standards; skills related to project management, critique, mentoring and coaching; attributes to support and sponsor your project and to make it possible for you to grow intellectually; and the personal skills and sensitivities that are responsive to your needs.

If supervisors are to fulfil all these roles, and if you are to complete your project on time, there will be a number of considerations to work through. It is much like the case of a house-building project. In that particular case, the project manager needs to establish ways in which the various tradespeople employed on the job will operate in order to see the project through to completion. The project manager certainly does not want to witness any friction amongst the tradespeople or see any of them walking off the job. His or her key objective is to get the house built. A good working relationship on the house project site will ensure that happens, and good working relationships develop from shared understanding between all parties concerning how the parties will operate.

In the supervision arrangement, the first supervisor typically assumes the role of project manager. It is the first supervisor who is the linchpin in the project. He or she will want to be sure that the most effective supervision arrangements are established to allow the project to proceed through to completion. Like the house project manager working with others, the first supervisor will seek the respective views of others participating in the project on how they wish to operate. Your own views will also be taken into account.

Together you and your supervisors will figure out the ground rules for how you will all work. Supervisors operate with different styles and methods and they need to agree amongst themselves what will work best. You, too, will want to be clear in the negotiation process about what approaches you consider would work best for you. Are you someone who blossoms with minimal guidance, or are you someone who needs strong direction and detailed feedback? Unless these differences are out in the open and negotiated, you could all find yourselves working towards different objectives.

"My ideal supervisor is somebody who gives you informed feedback when you get to that stage of your writing so that you have a clear idea of what it is that is good and working and those areas that really do need additional thought and rework. Somebody who is available and approachable. Someone who can give you feedback in a timely manner."

Meetings and correspondence are major considerations in your early negotiations. How frequently will you meet? Where will you meet and for what duration each time? Will you meet online, or face to face, or both? Will your communication be confined to formal meetings or will it also involve informal encounters? How will you be able to communicate minor concerns of the project? By phone? Will you correspond through email? Will all parties in the supervision arrangement be able to see the correspondence? Will you provide your supervisors with regular updates of your work and minutes of meetings? How frequently will you report on progress? Will you be the person responsible for setting the agenda for each meeting? Who will chair the meetings?

Then there are the expectations of work: the goals, the deadlines and the feedback. These decisions are agreed amongst you all. From your research proposal timeline you will have a clear idea of what you want to complete within a specific period of time. However, your timeline is up for negotiation with your supervisors and, on their advice, you may need to consider revising it. Will your supervisors want regular writing from you? If so, all of you will need to be clear of the expectations concerning the specific content, the word count and time frame. What are your supervisors proposing by way of feedback? Will they all be involved in reviewing the first full draft? What about publications resulting from the project? Will supervisors expect to be named as co-authors?

"I think when we were able to communicate honestly, things worked well. Knowing that you were going to get feedback on whatever you put in was always an important part of that relationship. When it did happen it was good."

Projects that proceed successfully to completion do so without unnecessary confusion over expectations. Many universities require supervisors and students to formalise working arrangements through a written contract. Even if your university does not require a contractual arrangement, it is always useful to draw up a statement of expectations. When you and your supervisors comply with the terms of your working relationship as outlined in your statement of expectations, the project is more likely to proceed smoothly. In the unlikely event of things going wrong, your contractual obligations as specified in the statement will be a particularly useful resource for resolving issues between parties.

"My ideal supervisor is someone who cares, and has a genuine interest in you doing well, who is very supportive, who can understand that there needs to be structure associated with the supervision process. By that I mean there needs to be some sort of guidelines about what's expected of you."

Making the supervision arrangement work

When you and your supervisors are agreed on the terms of your working relationship, your efforts within the relationship will be taken for granted by your supervisors. Given that their commitment to your project is one of their many academic responsibilities, there are likely to be very real difficulties within the supervision arrangement if you do not honour the contractual agreement. Develop a sensitivity that your supervisor, like any other professional, has a range of work responsibilities in addition to your supervision, and, in the supervision relationship, irrespective of the friendliness and collegiality it demonstrates, the supervisor is always in a more influential position within the supervisor/student hierarchy.

While you need to demonstrate consistent effort throughout the entire project, keep in mind that your supervisors' involvement will be more intensive during some stages of the project. As the nature of the work changes over the course of the project, and as your maturity as a researcher develops, the nature of the supervision relationship is likely to change. Supervision operates in a dynamic space. At all stages, however, it is important that you maintain your working relationship, even if it is simply to keep your supervisors informed of what you are doing in your project.

"Where my supervisors have been particularly proactive is in the sense of the sorts of things I should consider – perhaps other resources that might be helpful to illuminate areas that I might be struggling with. And sometimes just to talk things out with them. If I had a particular issue or a particular

struggle I could talk with them and it didn't have to be necessarily in a formal supervision meeting but just down in the coffee room having a chat at morning tea and just bring something up. It was an opportunity to try and sort out what it was I was thinking about in terms of, say, here is the theory and here is my research and this is what I am finding in my data and how does that connect to the theory? Those kinds of informal conversations I found really helpful."

At supervision meetings, honouring your side of the bargain means that you give your supervisors the courtesy of observing the social conventions of a formal institutionalised social arrangement. It means that you will need to take care that your involvement in the relationship remains at all times at the professional level. It should go without saying that a romantic association is inappropriate. Such a relationship is likely to create major problems for you with regard to relationships with others who have an involvement with your work. More significantly, there could well be aspersions cast on the authenticity of your work.

Your professional responsibilities in the supervision relationship require you to be punctual for meetings and to be well prepared. Supervisors are permitted to be late but you are not. If you are given the opportunity to set the agenda and chair the meeting, circulate the agenda ahead of time and focus the discussion on achieving the objectives of that agenda. Of course there is scope for friendly chit-chat at the meeting and such informal discussion will assist the supervisors in coming to know you in a broader context. However, the doctoral research activity needs to remain the key focus.

Good preparation is important if you hope to negotiate your move from dependent learner to independent researcher. Be sure that you have completed the objectives you set out for the meeting and provide your supervisors with a brief written account of how you met the objectives. Give your supervisors plenty of time to read the progress report and any other written work well before the set meeting. At the meeting tell the supervisors in your own words how you are progressing and the small breakthroughs you have made. Let them also know of any issues you encountered and tell them what you have done to resolve those issues. Your supervisors will appreciate honesty and are fully aware that research is often uncertain and ambiguous. They will particularly want to know how issues have been resolved. If, through your efforts, solutions were not forthcoming then ask for specific advice and guidance.

There is likely to be a raft of questions that need answers, including those related to academic knowledge, to writing, to support, to doctoral conventional practice. Supervisors do not expect you will necessarily know at the beginning of your doctoral journey, for example, which researchers are leading the field, which journals are less prominent in your area, how to use the Internet to best effect, or how to set out a thesis. As you progress through the journey, your questions may become more focused on specific challenges, such as how to marshal sound arguments in the analysis processes. Questions will arise at every level precisely because there is no prescribed training or formula for undertaking doctoral study. You will learn through the process. No matter how inconsequential your question might seem to you, be sure that you share your concerns and queries with your supervisors who will assist you with both practical and academic guidance.

Of course, some questions carry a greater significance than others. Take, for example, the question of whether or not to change the direction of your project. Gradually, you may have come to feel uncomfortable with the current plan. If that is the case, then your supervisors will need to know of your changed thinking as soon as possible, and preferably before the new plan is fully developed, so that they can contribute to the dialogue that will, first, establish a need for a new direction, and second, assist in the shaping and support of the new direction. A changed direction may throw current support structures out of kilter, so be sure that you all discuss your new intentions early on. Mostly, however, students do not consider making wholesale changes to their research plan. Most changes made to the plan are more modest and supervision sessions are able to remain focused on advancing the thesis through an original or slightly modified plan.

Supervision sessions are set up to advance the thesis. When supervision sessions advance the thesis through discussion and debate of complex ideas, the experience is often an exhilarating one for all involved.

Case study

Jim's professional relationship with his supervisors was especially enriching. As Jim said, 'It was incredibly enjoyable bouncing ideas with them. We'd be able to come up with gems that we wouldn't have been able to come up with without each other.' The secret to the success, Jim believed, was that they all came to an issue from a different angle. They also knew when to leave the others alone and when to connect again. Jim would contact the supervisors and let them know he had an idea and when they were ready to talk it through with him they would get back together again.

Advancing ideas through the supervision meeting is extremely productive for all parties concerned. Such meetings are places where you are likely to develop a sense of belonging to the community of professional researchers. Unlike your previous experiences of teaching and learning structures in which you listened, watched and learned, the supervision meeting is more collegial and more balanced in participant contribution. You and your supervisors all learn from the academically 'charged' thinking that is shared and from the collaborative explorations that take place. Establishing an environment that explores a range of ideas may not, however, come easily to your supervisors. It may require a level of creativity on your part which, in turn, you can offer by putting both well-conceived and underdeveloped ideas forward as a starting point for discussion at the meeting. Like most things in life, you will derive more satisfaction from the supervision meetings when you contribute more of your effort.

In order to scaffold your journey as a professional researcher, supervisors will read your written work and provide constructive feedback on it on a regular basis. Providing work for assessment is important because it keeps your supervisors in tune with your thinking and with what is happening. Perhaps you have initiated the assessment – in which case, identify what feedback you require. For example, perhaps you might want to know if you have interpreted a theoretical standpoint correctly. Perhaps you seek views on the argument you present. Be warned that many supervisors do not take kindly to being asked to focus on grammar, spelling and general language. They will want you to carry out the editing before you send them the writing, which will then allow them to focus on the content matter. If you need assistance with English, then you should seek out such assistance from a writing support group.

Whatever reasonable feedback you require, the feedback you receive will be directed towards structuring and advancing your professional identity. However, most students feel particularly vulnerable when waiting for feedback and, if you feel likewise, chances are you will be seeking reassurance that your work is on the right track. You may be sufficiently confident with your efforts and be seeking out praise but be mindful that, in order for you to grow intellectually, praise needs to be aligned with quality feedback that assists you in enhancing the quality of the work.

Constructive feedback is sometimes misinterpreted by students. One student might over-react to critique, believing that the supervisor is outrageously wrong. Another student might believe that the feedback is signalling that they, the student, are not of the calibre for doctoral study. Both reactions need careful consideration. First, supervisors are providing a viewpoint from experience and from knowledge of the field. While part of their critique might be questionable, they are not likely to be outrageously wrong. It is more likely that you based your work on a number of assumptions that have not been made clear to the reader. Your work may not have clarified your thinking adequately. You may not have made the intended links for the reader.

You may well have overlooked important literature. You might have given undue prominence to a particular aspect. Before you give expression to your initial heightened reactions, calmly let your supervisors know that you will give some serious consideration to their feedback. With careful attention to what the supervisors recommend, you may come to the realisation that in order to move the project forward you may need to rework a section or chapter. In that case, take care to store the deleted content in a new file. The material may come in useful in a later section.

Alternatively, in responding to feedback, you may feel strongly that your ideas do merit inclusion in the thesis. Even as your supervisor is endeavouring to broaden your ideas and knowledge, he or she is also hoping to push you towards more independent engagement with academic ideas. Hence, you do not need to accept supervisors' feedback as a directive for change. No supervisor wants a student to be a mere conduit for his or her own ideas and approach, just as no supervisor believes that he or she is the fountain of all knowledge. You must feel ownership of the thesis and this means that you must be prepared to discuss and debate the feedback provided. Discussion involving all parties in the supervision process will likely point to a resolution and will give you an opportunity to make good any shortcomings. Remember in the discussion to define and defend your ideas to your supervisors, just as you define and defend your ideas to your thesis reader. Your notes of the discussion at the meeting can be summarised and circulated as minutes to the supervisors. They will also serve as a reminder of action points for you to follow up.

This brings us to the second point: that critique from the supervisor serves as an indicator that you are not of the calibre for doctoral study. The point is totally misguided. Do not forget that your acceptance into the doctoral programme attests to your capabilities to carry out doctoral work. One thing you need to be absolutely clear about is that it is perfectly natural, at times during the doctoral journey, to feel insecure in your own abilities. For sure, there will be some unexpected exhilarating stages and some reasonably predictable occurrences, but there will be other times when things do not proceed according to plan, when you cannot seem to make headway, when you identify that you lack a technological (or other) skill that is fundamentally important to progress, when the data do not conform to expectation, when the writing does not flow, when the workload is overwhelming and when you feel distinctly isolated. There are, too, for some students, personal problems associated with extreme health or life challenges. None of these challenges signals that doctoral study is inappropriate for you.

In moments of crises like these, take time out from the problem to tackle some more mechanical aspect of the thesis, such as checking references.

Importantly, do not avoid your supervisor but, instead, be sure that your supervisor is informed as soon as possible of the problems. He or she will not be able to provide the intense emotional support that you might feel you are in need of at the time. For that support you will need to seek out family or friends or persons more qualified to offer that assistance. But what your supervisor will be willing to do is offer encouragement and interest in your work, as well as the opportunity to talk things through with a view towards finding a solution. Talking through the issue may result in setting up modified objectives for the next phase of the project. It may result in establishing support mechanisms to assist in the development of a new skill. It may simply be a matter of collegial discussion to pave a way forward. It may, for the health- or life-challenged student, involve taking necessary leave of absence from the study. All these approaches will help you deal with the issues.

> *"Others who were doing their PhDs were helpful in telling me what they had come across – you know, issues that they had to address – and I found it all incredibly helpful just knowing that some of these things were just part and parcel of the process."*

● Resolving supervision issues

Changes in the supervision team do occur. Human factors that intervene often arise when a supervisor takes extended leave, resigns, retires or is confronted with major illness. These are all situations completely beyond the control of the student and, apart from health-related issues, the supervisor would be expected to inform the student early on of any imminent change to circumstances so that institutional processes can be initiated for the appointment of a new supervisor. A change of the student's research direction may also require a change of supervision. Typically, the first situation entails a replacement of supervisor while the second situation involves the addition to the supervision team with appropriate new expertise. There is a third situation, too, and that arises from an unsatisfying relationship amongst the parties in the supervision arrangement. In all three situations the experience takes its toll on the student's work, and the terms of the working relationship may need to be changed.

> *"My first supervisor had been ill and was away from the university for long periods, and there were long periods when I had no contact with her. So my second supervisor quite often would pick up and we would have meetings and it became more of a pattern."*

Students involved in the first situation generally feel that their work has been stalled, that their sense of isolation is made more acute, and, in some cases, feel severely let down by what they interpret as an apparent lack of care and support for the project on the supervisor's part. The prospect of working with another supervisor after having invested time and energy into developing the previous relationship is daunting. If this situation applies to you, it is important to establish the new working relationship as soon as possible. Your wider support group will help you make the transition productively. If your supervision panel has been added to, then you will require some level of adjustment to the new supervisor's perspectives and ways of operating. A new statement of expectations to accommodate the changed arrangements may need to be mutually agreed upon.

Consider the third situation, in which an unproductive relationship amongst the parties in the supervision process exists. As we all know, it is always more difficult to work productively with someone with whom you do not personally connect or who you believe does not show the interest you expect of your project at your meetings. Changing your supervisor or, alternatively, pretending to yourself that the conflict is not real may not be the most appropriate ways to deal with differences in temperament, approach and style. These are not academic issues and, as such, might easily be addressed in other ways. Talk with a trusted friend or colleague and brainstorm possible solutions. Then you will need to air your concerns, tactfully but openly, at your next meeting, pointing out what you perceive as a clash of personalities or interests and a possible solution.

Let us suppose the personal differences cannot be addressed in a mutually agreeable manner, or that the mismatch is of an academic nature and relates to perceived supervision inadequacies or negligent practices. You feel strongly that a change of supervision needs to be initiated.

Case study

Stephen's supervision experience started off on a good note. Both his supervisors were enthusiastic about his topic and were keen for him to succeed. The first supervisor's institutional responsibilities, however, slowly began to intrude on the supervision she was able to provide. The second supervisor tried to compensate for the first supervisor's sporadic involvement when he realised that progress on the project was stalling. He set up meetings with Stephen to offer advice and feedback because he wanted to be sure that things were ticking along and that Stephen was on track for completion. However, the first supervisor resented the second supervisor's interference in what she perceived was her role as first supervisor. It became a very difficult situation for Stephen. He seriously considered talking with the ➡

director of the doctoral programme because, as he explained, 'it was getting to the position where I was the meat in the sandwich and I did not feel comfortable in the situation'. While he was deliberating about what he should do, the first supervisor announced she was retiring and the issue was resolved amongst the three parties. The second supervisor then stepped up to become first supervisor and a new second supervisor was appointed.

If the problem does not resolve itself, there are formal institutional policies and processes available to you which will take some of the load off your shoulders. In the first instance, begin by talking confidentially with and seeking advice from the head of your academic unit. If the issue is not able to be resolved at this level using the head of unit as a mediator, then your case can be referred on to a higher authority within the institution.

Conflict within the supervision arrangement is reasonably rare. Be assured that almost all supervisors are keen to establish processes and create arrangements that will enhance your doctoral experience. They very much want you to succeed. They offer their knowledge and experience and provide support at a wide range of levels designed for your personal growth and intellectual development. They want to create an experience for you that is both enriching and productive. The level at which you take advantage of the support on offer is up to you, of course.

In the next chapter our focus will be on writing the doctoral thesis. We explore the skills that you will need to develop in order to demonstrate your competence in producing a scholarly, relevant and contemporary account of a study at a level appropriate to doctoral study. The importance of identifying your standpoint and of clarifying your specific contribution to the wider research discipline is emphasised.

Review

Main points:
- Doctoral study is a shared responsibility.
- Your university, the library, your colleagues and peers provide you with support for you to succeed.
- Your intellectual development is enhanced by the research culture at your university.

- The most influential form of support will almost certainly be provided by your supervisor.
- Supervisor selection is crucial to doctoral success.
- Supervisors provide human, infrastructural and material resources to enhance your learning.
- The terms of the working relationship are agreed by all parties involved with the supervision.
- Constructive feedback from supervisors on your work is essential to advance your project.
- Changes to the supervision do sometimes occur due to circumstances beyond the control of the student.
- Formal institutional policies are available to resolve major supervision issues.

Key terms:
- Institutional policies, regulations and codes of conduct for doctoral study
- Monitoring progress
- Support for personal growth and intellectual development
- Supervisor selection
- Statement of expectations
- Scaffolding your journey
- Constructive feedback
- Resolving differences

7 Getting on with Writing

This chapter looks at:

▶ The importance of writing
▶ Structures and conventions
▶ The thesis argument
▶ The purposes of the main sections within a thesis
▶ Enhancing the communication between writer and reader
▶ Preparing for thesis submission

The importance of writing

Writing is a major component of doctoral work. Considering that your doctoral thesis is likely to be substantially bigger than anything you have previously written, you can be excused for feeling daunted by the prospect of stretching your writing skills to reach the word count. But put things in perspective. To reach this stage in your student life you have already demonstrated your competence at writing. Take a moment to reflect on the vast number of assignments and essays you have written as a student in which you communicated ideas in an academic way. As a doctoral candidate, you will have already moved through the first writing hoops with your research proposal and have a clear sense of the various parts of your thesis. In the course of preparing your proposal, you will have written a short first draft of your introduction, a short first draft of your literature review and a description of your methodology. Let's face it: you are well underway with your thesis writing.

In the course of writing your proposal you would have found that you were thinking deeply as you were going. The writing sparked thoughts and enabled you to make sense of and clarify what you were proposing to do in your study. Another way of saying that is that your thinking was enhanced when you began to express your ideas through the writing process. You started with a few rough thoughts in your head and, as you wrote, these then crystallised or moved off in other directions, developing and creating ideas that were sensible and coherent. That is why is it so important to commit your thoughts to writing as soon as possible.

Many doctoral candidates speak of the writing stage as the period of time and the task they do when they have collected and analysed their data. Procrastinating your writing until after the data analysis and during the final months before your thesis submission deadline is far from ideal. You can be sure that the writing will take a lot longer than you anticipate. It involves lots of drafts and revising – so, if you want to produce your most polished effort, and if you want to discover and learn from the writing, you need to write as you go. Getting started will not be so difficult if you build on the early drafts you developed in your proposal.

> **"**The best advice I got while I was writing the thesis was from my supervisor, who kept telling me: focus on getting it written rather than getting it right.**"**

Everyone will be keen to give you advice, and you may want to seek advice widely. However, seeking advice widely is not altogether productive and you should consult your supervisor. Be careful to avoid approaching potential examiners because engagement with your work before examination will exclude them from the examination process. When seeking advice, remember that what works for some people might not work for you. The important thing is to face up to what is likely to get in the way of your writing. It might be a matter of scheduling in regular time for writing and setting manageable goals and realistic deadlines for a piece of writing. Perhaps you like an environment where you can see and hear others rather than be hidden away in a distraction-free work space. Is your preference for a clear or a cluttered desk? Do you work best when you can tick off daily writing tasks on a to-do list? Perhaps you like to reward yourself when a bit-sized piece is completed. How do you begin a new chapter? Do you spend time jotting down a few ideas, key words or phrases and then work them together in a way that ignores all the rules of academic prose before attending to rules of prose writing? Perhaps you like to focus on grammar, sentence and paragraph structure right from the start. Once you minimise the negative factors and focus on creating arrangements and conditions that will be conducive to your writing, your confidence in your own writing abilities will develop.

Activity

1. Write as many entries as you can to complete the table. Use more lines if required.

Factors that impede my writing	Factors that support my writing

2. Write down how you plan to minimise the negative and maximise the positive factors.

A thesis will do its best to take over your thinking. This is not a bad thing, of course. The problem is capturing those brilliant ideas that pop into your head at unexpected moments. You might be in the midst of writing – but you might equally be doing something completely different such as driving the car, eating dinner or drifting off to sleep! Have a strategy, such as notebook and pen, electronic tablet or journal at the ready, to capitalise on the inspirational moment. Recording your ideas, whether they are invited or otherwise, will be instrumental in the development of your thinking for the thesis. Interestingly, you will be surprised at the way your thinking develops and changes over the course of the writing.

There are a number of avenues you can explore to seek assistance with your writing. You can check out examples of effective academic writing from your own reading and you can learn from those examples. You might also want to see what support your university offers, in addition to your supervision arrangements. Many universities have structures in place that provide writing support. Take advantage of these. There are also more informal support groups that often develop amongst doctoral students.

> *"Writing skills is the first thing that I want to improve. I have been helping myself and going to the student development centre and I ask people to help me out. The writing consultant is not only helping me to edit my writing but sometimes if I start with an idea I can talk with him. Also some of my PhD colleagues have been studying in the same area so I talk with them and usually I get some good ideas back, some suggestions, some advice."*

More formal support group meetings amongst colleagues are usually scheduled at regular intervals and the group will develop an agreed-upon process for providing critical feedback to your writing. They will also develop informal processes for sharing concerns, doubts you have, or a stumbling block within your work. The group need not be composed of students from your own discipline area but each will need to share your interest in supporting others. Talking through these problems with a support group drawn from a range of experiences can often open up possible solutions. If you seek feedback and support, bear in mind that you must also be prepared to give constructive feedback to others.

You might use the group to test out a few writing ideas, or you might want to receive feedback on a small piece of writing. Some writing groups will expect you to read out loud the piece of writing you seek feedback on. Difficult though this might be at first, it is an excellent way of highlighting problems to do with listener engagement, grammar, syntax, tone, repetitiveness, sentence length, monotony and the like. It is also a way of establishing whether your writing flows in a logically organised and confident manner.

Ask yourself if there a sense of coherence between the ideas presented within the piece. You might want to consider reading sections out loud to yourself in the comfort of your own work space to check these issues.

What about those times when there is not a lot to show for your deep thinking? Any doctoral student will tell you that there will be days when the writing simply skips along. Then there are the 'other days'. Here is a suggestion for those 'other days': as you complete a writing session, write a note setting out a small and realistic objective for when you return to the writing. On return, check over what you wrote last session, remind yourself of your objective for this session and spend a short time weighing up approaches that might achieve that objective. If the writing is still not forthcoming, then choose another activity related to your research, such as completing progress forms for your institution, or checking references. At all costs, avoid wasting your precious study time on unrelated tasks.

> **"**The biggest challenge for me to overcome is that whole enormous shift from science research and science writing to social science writing. What have I done about it? Well, apart from talking to other people, I've made extensive use of the library and the compulsory readings and the recommended reading lists. And I've been getting out some of those other books and looking at what they had to say about writing style because it is so different. I don't know how many papers I've read but I've read what feels like millions and you start to get a feel for it … but it takes a long time.**"**

Structures and conventions

The thing that you are really trying to do through your writing is communicate your research to others. Communication, in any form, is played by a set of rules. Take the example of driving a car. As a driver, you follow a set of road rules relevant to your locality and every other competent driver in that same locality does the same. Since everyone knows what is expected of you and you know what is expected of other drivers, getting from A to B is a relatively easy exercise for everyone. Communication between the writer and reader of a doctoral thesis is much the same. Readers, especially examiners, expect you to communicate in a particular way. They expect a certain structure. When these expectations are met, getting from the start to the finish of your thesis will be a relatively easy exercise for the reader.

Of course, there are many other things besides a clear structure that readers hope for in your writing. They will appreciate a number of technical aspects such as wide margins, double spacing and consistent font type and font size. They will be expecting you to apply standard English grammatical rules, using an academic genre, so you need to avoid clichés, jargon, abbreviated forms of words such as 'won't', expletives, as well as offensive language. They will be anticipating that your quotations support rather than establish or summarise a point you want to make and will expect to see appropriate attribution given for those quotations. They will expect to see references presented in the conventional form for the discipline, such as in APA. Depending on the discipline, they will accept the use of 'I' but would not react so favourably to the use of 'we' and 'us'.

All these factors contribute to a successful communication between you and the reader. But in terms of 'big picture' communication between you and the reader, it will be the headings used in the thesis that will shine light on what is in store for the reader. There will be some overlap with the headings used in your research proposal and, given that you are reporting on research that has already been undertaken (rather than proposed, as in the research proposal), the tense in the final thesis will change from future to past in some of the chapters. Allowing for some variation depending on your discipline and the topic area under investigation, and on possible regulations for doctoral thesis presentation within your institution (you will need to check these out), the thesis will generally cover a number of areas, as listed below. These areas will not necessarily become the title of respective chapters since often content-specific headings will be more informative. Whatever headings are used, broadly speaking, the areas that are likely to be covered are:

- Title
- Abstract
- Acknowledgements
- Table of contents
- Introduction
- Literature review/Theoretical framework
- Research methodology
- Findings or Results
- Discussion
- Conclusion
- References
- Appendices

The areas included in the thesis, when presented like this, seem to suggest that students work through the writing systematically from beginning to end. In fact, very few students do the writing in a sequential fashion. For example, it would be pointless to write the final version of your table of contents with page numbers until you had completed the thesis. That is not to suggest that you should avoid writing a draft table of contents, without page numbers, of course. A draft will be extremely important for focusing your writing. Most students like to begin with a chapter that is relatively straightforward, such as the literature review or the methodology chapter, and will develop their chapter from – and expand on – what they wrote of those sections in their research proposal.

When your tentative chapter headings for each chapter have been established, keep a poster of them in view in your work place. The list of headings is not meant to scare you with all the things that need to be done; it is simply meant to provide an overview of the entire thesis in order to keep you focused. Clearly, the content under some of these headings will be relatively short while the content under others will be substantial. However, all main headings are there to guide the reader and, in order to signal their importance in the structure of the thesis, they are often written in upper case and in bold.

Let us turn our attention to the content within chapter headings (e.g., Introduction; Literature review/Theoretical framework; Research design; Findings or Results; Discussion; Conclusion). It will be necessary to break up the extensive content under these main headings for ease of reading. You will also want to create breaks for introducing new themes. This is typically done with sub-headings, which are often broken up further with sub-sub-headings. In addition to the verbal headings, students often use numbering systems to make distinctions between the content matter. Obviously, there needs to be a clear link between similar parts of a numbering system. While divisions are often necessary within a chapter, it is important to keep in mind that too many layers of headings tend to suggest a lack of cohesion within a chapter.

We will look now at how one student used the verbal and numbering system jointly. In a case study earlier, in Chapter 2, Kirsten was planning on exploring truancy. She has now begun a first draft of the structure of her first chapter, which she plans to include in the **TABLE OF CONTENTS** (she used caps). When she writes her first chapter she will use lower case and bold font for the sub-headings (e.g., **1.1 Background and context)**, and lower case and italics font for the sub-sub-headings (e.g., *1.1.1 The educational contract*).

Kirsten took some time over the development of the chapter structure. The more she read, the more ideas she thought she needed to include in her chapter. How they all fitted together seemed a mystery but her writing group suggested, as a start, that she jot down everything that seemed important to include and then defend the inclusion of each. Once she had identified the items for inclusion in the chapter, she asked the group to help her talk through the relationships between each item. She found it easier to put her ideas on a

---

Example chapter

TOPIC: Truancy in primary schools within the United Kingdom
STUDENT: Kirsten

CHAPTER 1: INTRODUCTION

1.1 Background and context
  1.1.1 The educational contract
  1.1.2 State, school and family responsibilities

1.2 Significance and rationale for the study
  1.2.1 The implications for truant students on their citizenship capacity
  1.2.2 The implications for truant students on their future employment
  1.2.3 The implications for truant students of unstructured and unsupervised activity

1.3 How this research will explore the issue of truancy
  1.3.1 The research design
  1.3.2 Who will be involved

1.4 Foreshadowing the contents of the thesis

---

large piece of paper and draw connecting lines between items to illustrate major and minor relationships. After much discussion and crossing-out as well as additions of lines, she produced a concept map with which she was satisfied. From the concept map she was able to draw up her chapter structure.

Kirsten posted her draft structure on her office wall. As she got into the job of writing she found that the basic structure helped her organise her writing and allowed her to keep hold of the chapter's 'big picture'. She also found that once she started writing, her thoughts developed further so that the draft structure was not exactly what she finally presented. As a case in point, she found that she could create a stronger argument by combining the two sub-sub-sections 1.2.1 and 1.2.2. Completing the final version of the chapter and ticking it off her wall poster gave her a sense of immense accomplishment.

● The thesis argument

Writers communicate more successfully with their readers at the doctoral level when they present a carefully developed argument. Indeed, the hallmark of a scholarly thesis is an argument that is sufficiently convincing to contribute to new knowledge within your field of study. In scholarly terms, when you present an argument, you create a discussion around information and a series of claims related to that information. You substantiate those claims with compelling evidence from data or other sources and draw the threads of the discussion together by noting the relevance of your point of view. What you are trying to do in developing an argument is to persuade the reader to align their view of a problem or issue with yours. However, as we know from everyday life, people are not easily persuaded. Thesis readers are possibly even more sceptical. Persuasive arguments establish credibility by offering clarity and, more specifically, by providing a chain of reasoning for the reader, tracing a logical pathway that leads towards acceptance of the points being made.

Individual sentences and clusters of sentences are the key mechanism by which you build communication and engagement with your argument for your reader. No student can craft a clear argument without paying attention to the functions and conventions of paragraphs. The function of a paragraph is to create a deliberate break or pause to signal that you are introducing a new discussion into a section. You may take several paragraphs to complete the full discussion of your argument, at which point you will draw all the discussion threads together for the reader.

Let us now look at the conventions associated with paragraph writing. Paragraphs related to a specific point must be presented in a logical order. The overarching message or the point you want to convey to the reader is known as the topic sentence. There is only one key message presented through the topic sentence in a paragraph and that message is succinct and clearly expressed, and easily grasped by your reader. Avoid saying too much in your paragraph. If you offer the reader more than one topic sentence, the reading becomes confusing. You should shift a new idea to form a new paragraph if the idea warrants its own discussion. Otherwise, delete it. Often, but not always, the topic sentence that outlines the point you wish to make will be placed near the beginning or the end of the paragraph. All the other sentences within the paragraph will have a logical connection with the key idea expressed in your topic sentence. Some of the supporting sentences will complement your key idea. Other sentences will set out the relevance of your argument.

We will apply the rules of paragraph writing to the presentation of an argument. When developing your main argument you are likely to need several paragraphs, perhaps even sections, to get your point across. Do not assume that the reader is already aware of all the points you wish to make. Your points need to be spelt out carefully in a process akin to guided discovery. Take the reader slowly along with you. Do not put in too much of significance or too many fundamentals before the reader is ready for it. Rather than giving away too much too early you should build your argument up slowly.

Along the way you will offer supporting sentences that emphasise and complement your argument more strongly or that contradict your view. The way to craft a discussion that integrates your points with those of others is to provide evidence from authoritative sources within the literature or concrete or practical examples from other relevant sources to substantiate your argument; as well, you can offer counter-examples to set up a contradiction which you will then refute. To do this you could use a combination of direct quotes and paraphrasing.

What you particularly want to avoid is a situation in which readers feel they are being led through a succession of interesting ideas during which the writer assumes, incorrectly, that the links are obvious. You will need to be explicit about how each piece of evidence progressively supports (or does not support) your argument. Be clear whether or not you are aligning yourself with the various views you put forward. Is the evidence from others obviously right, obviously wrong, or just in line with your preferences? On what basis has the evidence been selected? Is it because it marks out the same territory as you? Weaving of your argument into the discussion and sequencing the examples carefully will be vital for readers to feel they are in command of your thinking. Developing a logical sequence of moves and stages will help you develop a sharper argument that is responsive to your reader. The supporting sequences will then lead to an establishment of the relevance of the point you are making with your overall thesis argument.

Since you are not yet considered an expert in the field, take care with the tone in which you present your argument. At the same time, you don't want to appear too deferential. You will need to maintain a humble-yet-confident register consistently throughout. But making a persuasive case involves more than tone. It involves writing a narrative that will capture the imagination of the reader, responding to an anticipated level of critique. The successful writer marshals sound arguments and, in the process, turns complex ideas into elegant and easily accessible arguments.

● The purposes of the main sections within a thesis

You can create a stronger argument in each of your thesis chapters when you know precisely what the purpose of the chapter is. You might not have thought about it in this way, but each of the main sections within a thesis has a defined purpose. It might be to set the scene or to describe what you actually did and found. Or it might be to examine evidence or to offer an interpretation, and so on. Writing the chapter in a way that responds to the purpose will provide better communication between you and the reader. By shifting your focus onto the purpose and what the reader wants and expects from each chapter, your research will become more accessible.

Let us look in some detail at the purposes of individual content areas:

Title: The title is expected to clarify concisely what your investigation is about. Choose your words carefully to offer a compelling and succinct description of your work.

Abstract: The abstract is expected to encapsulate in a few short paragraphs, often around 300 words, the topic area, the research methods and the major findings, as well as the significance of the findings.

Acknowledgements: The purpose of the acknowledgements is to allow you to pay formal recognition to institutions and people who have assisted you in some way during your research journey. Your supervisors are obvious candidates for formal acknowledgement, but so too are family members, friends and others who have supported you in other ways.

Table of contents: The table of contents is the means by which the reader first discovers what each of the chapters will include. It offers more detail about the content of the thesis than the summary form of the abstract. Just like the example above that set out the sub-headings and sub-sub-headings for an introduction chapter, the table of contents will include that same level of detail for all the chapters and will also include page numbers. Lists of Tables and Lists of Figures, if used, should also be included following on from the chapter detail. You might also need to include a Glossary of Terms and a List of Abbreviations or acronyms used in the thesis.

Introduction: The introduction is designed to set the scene for your research, provide a rationale for the study, and briefly summarise the content of succeeding chapters. An identification of the problem or issue under investigation usually comes early in the chapter and is supported by background information that makes it possible for the reader to see why the specific topic was chosen and why the study needs to be undertaken. The introduction is written in such a way that the reader gets a clear sense of what the research is all about, and, without too much detail, the methodology chosen and the participants (or subject matter), as well as what the contribution to knowledge will be. The reader also becomes aware of what is in store within the succeeding chapters.

Literature review/Theoretical framework: The literature review is intended to reveal to the reader that your reading is relevant, up to date, and well chosen to align with your own work and to demonstrate that you are capable of adding a contribution to this body of work. It is to show that you can engage with, synthesise and critique the current knowledge base in your area and to reveal that there is an opening for you within that knowledge base for your proposed study. Key concepts, terms and expressions are defined and often the research questions will be presented, following on directly from the opening you have identified within the literature for your research.

In this chapter you may also want to set your work within a theoretical framework. However, some students, depending on the kind of research being undertaken, choose to include a chapter specifically devoted to theoretical standpoint. Wherever you decide is the most appropriate place, your theoretical standpoint must be made transparent to the reader. It needs to illuminate the key ideas and concepts that will provide an indication in this chapter how your data are likely to be gathered and analysed.

Research methodology: The purpose of the methodology chapter is to describe what you have done in your study and to provide a justification for the choices made, offering sound reasons for not choosing other options to address your research questions. Your decisions should be explained in such a way that another researcher is absolutely clear about the assumptions underpinning those decisions and would be able to replicate the study. Since the chapter needs to clarify the research design and the ways in which you implemented that design, you will need to set out clearly your methods of data collection and analysis, and provide details of the research setting and the selection of participants involved. The chapter will also inform the reader of any problems encountered during the fieldwork, or any other problems – for example, those related to technology – and describe how these problems were addressed to ensure that the research was not compromised. The reader will also expect that ethical issues will be discussed here.

Findings or Results: The findings chapter will present research findings that are relevant to your research questions, without interpretation or analysis. However, if your kind of research warrants it, you may choose to combine a findings chapter with a discussion chapter, in which case the findings will be both reported and analysed in the same chapter. The presentation of a stand-alone findings chapter should be carefully structured through the use of text, tables, figures, images or diagrams, or through a combination of these forms. The reader will expect to see a clear data trail, with descriptions of 'who' and 'what' and explanations of 'when' and 'where'. If you use tables or figures, it is important that each is presented according to APA (or similar) style and that the data are explained to the reader through a textual presentation in addition to the visual presentation.

Discussion: The purpose of the discussion chapter is to relate your findings to previous research and theory. The chapter needs to demonstrate that you are able to summarise the main points, that you are able to make sense of the data and that you are able to provide a convincing argument that allows you to address the research questions. Since the intent is to establish where previous research is supported as well as where it is challenged, it is important to provide confirming or disputing evidence from your exploration of relationships within the data so that you can offer a basis for your claims in relation to support or challenge of the literature. It is also important to draw attention to any theoretical issues that have unfolded as a result of your research.

Conclusions: The overall purpose of the conclusions chapter is to confirm that your research warrants a doctoral qualification. It needs to demonstrate that the research you have done is credible, valid and relevant to the research setting and, importantly, in setting the work within the field, that it is clear that your research makes a contribution to knowledge. The chapter provides your reflections on the research process. It revisits the research questions and sums up the responses to those questions. It highlights your main findings and the major achievements of the work, discussing the significance of the study and, where appropriate, the relevance, implications and recommendations of the findings for policy or specific stakeholders. The reader needs to know what the limitations of the study are and what further research might be worth undertaking as a result of your findings. The reader may also welcome a short section in this chapter or in an afterword on your own journey in terms of skills and knowledge development and any early assumptions that changed through the process.

References: The purpose of the references is to acknowledge the ideas of others which you drew on in the thesis. References list all (but only those) references that were included in the thesis text. The text includes all authors referred to in the in-text citations, and, if used, the footnotes and the endnotes.

Appendices: The appendices are composed of additional material that is useful for the reader to know about. This body of material often includes ethics information letters, questionnaire or interview questions, and detailed statistical calculations. Each is presented with its own number so that it can be identified within the thesis text.

Having looked in detail at the main headings, it begins to become clear that there is a wide range of purposes for your writing within the thesis. Coming to grips with the purpose of the content under each of the main headings will allow you to appreciate what kind of information to provide, whether the tense of the discussion under the main heading will be past, present or future, and what approximate length the discussion needs to be. Being responsive to each of the main purposes of doctoral chapters allows you to consider each chapter as an important entity in its own right and, therefore, suitable for publication immediately, if your university permits thesis-by-publication, or in the future, if it does not. Getting the chapter ready for publication submission may require some additional work but the strong foundations will already be in place.

While getting published might well be an important objective for you, take care over what you commit to while working on your thesis. Remember that the completion of the thesis needs to remain your overriding concern as far as writing goes. Any additional writing for publication that you undertake should align with your topic area and should not stray too far away from the position that you take in the thesis. Some students become seduced by the prospect of publication and submit manuscripts on areas of interest that have little or nothing in common with the thesis. The preparation, the cognitive effort and the time involved in writing unrelated papers will put you behind in the completion stakes.

● Enhancing the communication between writer and reader

Now that we are familiar with what readers expect by way of thesis structure and argumentation, as well as chapter purpose, it is time to consider how you might present your writing in order to enhance communication between you and your reader. After all, if you can get the reader fully engaged with and interested in the thesis, then you are setting yourself up for certain success. Of course, our discussion on enhancing communication will presume that your content is of doctoral standard.

First impressions are extremely important to the reader. Many readers are able to conjure up their views of the quality of the thesis from the way you write the abstract and the introduction. They also like things to be made easy for them. As they journey through your writing they will expect to be able to navigate your work with the help of a roadmap and clear signposts. One easy way to provide that guided support is by introducing each new chapter with an overview of what the chapter is about, its objective and the structure of the chapter. This is particularly important, given the vastly different purposes within the thesis. Clarifying the chapter objective might seem obvious but it is surprising how many doctoral students choose to submerge their readers directly in the deep end without any signposting. You can also introduce each new section sub-heading with a discussion of the points you plan to write about, and you can conclude each section with a brief summary of the key points made within the section.

Consider using repetition as a strategy to remind your reader of an important point made in an earlier chapter within the thesis. You might even consider it necessary to use repetition within a chapter. The problem with not making the focus, intentions and key points of the chapter explicit is that readers may construct unintended meanings from the chapter or may not be able to forge the same connections that you do. The strategies suggested are designed to position your reader on the same wavelength as you with your work.

If you want your reader to be 'in tune' with you, the most obvious approach is to link the thesis together in a coherent way. Some readers will read the abstract and introduction and then leap ahead to the conclusion chapter. What they are looking for is coherence and a consistency in approach. They can determine whether or not your thesis is logically organised from your table of contents. They can quickly determine if the flow from one chapter to another is organised in such a way that one chapter follows naturally from the preceding chapter, or whether it is organised in a haphazard manner. Between chapters, a logically organised discussion will ensure that each chapter leads naturally into the next, so you will need to close each chapter with an explicit launching statement. The thesis will also need to be consistent in its structure, from one chapter to the next. This point also applies to the order in which information is presented, particularly in relation to the collection of data and the analyses of those data. The reader will expect that the data will be dealt with in the way they were originally presented in the findings chapter.

You can help your reader navigate through your work with the help of clear signposts. You might consider using parallelism so that the reader can develop understanding more quickly and be in tune with your thinking. An example will help here: 'Just as every student is required to study mathematics, so too every student should be required to study science.' Another acceptable approach is to provide the reader with the same kind of information in the body of the chapter as that offered in the introduction and the conclusion of the chapter. Some students get so carried away with writing the body of the chapter that they forget what they have promised in the introduction to the chapter.

Sentences need to make clear sense. Be sure that the subject and verb of the sentence are placed close together. Many students fall into the habit of starting a new sentence with 'this', such as in 'This created a problem ...', or 'This meant that ....' As a result, the reader is often left wondering what 'this' refers to. Clarify the antecedent. Good writing makes explicit who is doing what. Good writing uses transitions between sentences and shows how sentences are related. Smooth transitions are equally important between paragraphs. Clear transitional sentences or words such as 'additionally', 'subsequently' and 'on the other hand' are crucially important in the construction of an argument.

There are a number of other stepping-stones that you can offer your reader. Acknowledge all your sources. Make sure that your formatting is consistent and clear and that the complex ideas expressed through your writing are readily accessible. How many scholarly pieces have you read that are extraordinarily difficult to wade through? The difficulty could well be the result of the writer expressing too many ideas within a paragraph. If that is the case, it is likely that the sentences are long and rambling. Conciseness and simplicity are important. Just as readers do not appreciate overly long and complex sentences, they also do not appreciate sentences that are too brusque. Variation in sentence length is what they most welcome and what will generate their interest. Readers will also expect consistency in your chosen keywords and in the way you use terminology. No reader wants to experience confusion.

You may decide to delete specific words from your chapter. You will particularly want to cut out qualifiers (e.g., 'sort of', 'quite', 'very') and value words (e.g., 'bad', 'disastrous'), as well as strings of adjectives. You may decide to delete a sentence, a paragraph or even a section from your chapter. Keep it in another file just in case you decide to use it later. When you feel you have done your best to engage the reader at the chapter level, leave it for a while. Returning to it later, you will read it with fresh eyes. Then the chapter revision can begin.

● Preparing for thesis submission

If revision of your work is important at the chapter level, it is critically important at the level of the thesis. Many students underestimate the importance

Activity

Read through one completed chapter.

1. Check that you delivered what you promised in your chapter introduction.
2. Check that you conclude the chapter with a short summary of the ideas in the chapter.
3. Read the paragraphs in a section carefully. Is there one topic sentence in each paragraph?
4. Are all the sentences within each paragraph closely related to the topic sentence?
5. Have you used complex terminology when simple words would suffice?
6. Are the transitions between sentences and between paragraphs smooth?
7. Have you ended the chapter with a smooth lead into the next chapter?

of the thesis revision process and the time it takes to get the thesis ready for submission. It is as if the writing is finished once each individual chapter has been checked and revised. What they forget is that the thesis must have its own integrity, and, since the purposes of each chapter are unique, presenting a coherent piece of work is not entirely straightforward. There are other students, too, who are unwilling to let go of the writing and declare the first full draft finished.

Whether you cannot call the project finished – or cannot wait to call it finished – you will need to allow plenty of time for revision. You will find that the revision process is easier if you work from a hard copy of your thesis. Read it with critical eyes. Read what is actually on the page, not what you thought you had written. Start with the big picture and check the structure, looking for consistency across chapters. In the finer details, ask yourself if you have over- or under-explained an important point. Try not to be too precious about your wonderful work and be prepared to prune, elaborate or reorganise so that the reader will be able to share your meaning. When the writing has been revised, then you can begin to edit.

Your editing will need to pay attention to grammar and spelling and look for typographical errors. Do not rely on the spelling and grammar checks provided by the software on your computer! Be sure that your punctuation is correct, that you use apostrophes appropriately, and that your verb tenses match the purpose of the chapter. Check all your references. Most importantly, check for evidence of your habitual errors and correct them. Careless presentation is easy to avoid and it is critically important that you do avoid it because it tends to colour the reader's thinking into believing that the research, the data collection and analysis have also been undertaken carelessly.

Even if you consider your thesis ready for submission after revision and editing, seek the advice of your supervisors. They have the experience to assess whether your work reads as though your research was plausible, credible and trustworthy and, hence, whether it is at the submission stage. Regulations in some universities require you, at the time when you are getting close to submission, to give notice of your intention to submit. This typically involves the completion of a standard form confirming your plans to submit your thesis for examination. Most universities require that you submit a specific number of bound (either spiral or hard bound) copies of your thesis. Some universities will allow you to include in the submission your academic publications that support and are additional to your thesis work. Binding will take time so be sure that you plan for this part of the process. In the order of things, in the life of your thesis, submission is a monumental milestone. Savour the moment; then, if you have any energy left, take a break to do all those exciting activities you postponed until after submission.

In the next chapter we move to the time when the examination of the thesis is taking place. We learn that there are, typically, two aspects to the examination process: independent written assessments of your work from examiners and a defence or viva (oral examination). We look at how examiners make their assessments and what you need to prepare for in order to demonstrate your independence as a researcher.

Review

Main points:
- Writing is a major component of doctoral work, so do not procrastinate.
- Thinking is enhanced when you express your ideas through the writing process.
- Support groups can assist by offering constructive feedback on your writing.
- It is through your writing that you communicate your research to others.

- The main headings used in the thesis will signal how you have structured your work.
- A draft structure will help you organise your writing.
- An argument is the hallmark of a scholarly thesis.
- Each of the main sections in the thesis has a defined purpose.
- Each paragraph has only one key message.
- Clear transitional sentences or words will enhance a reader's engagement with your work.
- Do not underestimate the importance of thesis revision and the time it takes to prepare for submission.

Key terms:
- Communication with the reader
- Thesis argument
- Thesis submission

8 Getting Examined

● The examination process

At last the end is in sight! You have submitted your thesis and, in doing that, you and your supervisors are signalling that you are satisfied that the work is ready for examination. Following submission, the thesis will be on its way to and in the hands of the examiners. After years of perseverance, ups and downs, and, above all, genuine hard work on your part, you are finally on the home stretch to becoming a fully professional researcher in your chosen field.

Let us look at what happens in the examination process. The process typically involves two parts. It will involve independent written assessments of your work from examiners. In most institutions it will also involve a defence or viva (oral examination). The written thesis is the principal means by which you are identified as a competent researcher in the examiners' written reports. However, the viva or defence also contributes to the final assessment of your competence as a researcher. It takes place following the submission of the examiners' reports and represents the culminating event of the examination process.

It is important that you are fully aware of the procedures and processes within your university regarding thesis examination. In many universities, names of potential examiners will be considered by your supervisors, and possibly by the head of the department. It is quite possible you will be involved in that discussion, and your recommendations of potential examiners who you believe will provide a fair assessment of your work will be taken into account. In nominating examiners you should give some consideration to academics whose work you have cited in your thesis. Be mindful of their specific scholarly interests and consider how their work meshes with or is in contrast to yours. Be mindful too, that examiners who are inexperienced will not have read many theses but they may have the necessary expertise that other contenders do not have.

In your deliberations, you might want to take into account the fact that within some fields the status of the examiners is reflective of the quality of the examination. Another way of thinking about this is that the quality of the thesis is guaranteed by the quality of the examiners. If you are seeking to become a professional researcher, then gaining recognition and credibility from the careful and strategic selection of an eminent examiner may open a lot of doors for both your immediate plans and your future scholarly trajectory. Striking the right chord with your examiner may well be to your long-term advantage.

If you are not able to participate in the nomination of examiners, at the very least you will be given the opportunity to name any unsuitable examiners. Once examiners are decided upon, the procedure, then, in some institutions, is for the supervisors to approach the examiners informally to determine their availability to examine. When availability is confirmed the names are passed on to the institution. In many respects it will be helpful if you know the identity of your examiners and to have this information well before your thesis is submitted. It is helpful because if you have not already made reference to their publications in appropriate and relevant places within the thesis, you will have the opportunity and time to do so before the thesis is completed. Citing, quoting and discussing the work of your examiners in a way that enriches your work is always a good strategy.

There are likely to be three examiners who will assess your work. One may possibly be based within your own university, while the other two are likely to be external to your university. Most examiners are doctorally qualified. If not, they will have expertise and experience, usually within an applied field relevant to your work, at a level deemed appropriate for assessing your work. All three examiners will be involved in the wider area in which your research is situated. None of the examiners will have been involved in supervising your work. Nor should they have acted as an adviser in any capacity during the development of the thesis, or worked with you in any other research project.

Shortly after you submit your thesis the examiners will each receive a hard copy of it. Along with the thesis the university will provide advice on the examination procedures and on the format expected of the examination report. The examiners are each asked to provide a report which is reflective of his or her own views and which is not produced following consultation with any others. The report will usually note any changes that the examiner considers *mandatory* for an acceptable standard. The report will also note any *recommended* changes. Examiners are also asked to make an overall assessment recommendation on the basis of their reading of the thesis.

● The written thesis examination

If the mere mention of the word 'examination' makes you anxious, then take heart. Examiners, at the outset, do not entertain a view of you as an intruder, seeking uninvited entry into the researcher community. They do not look negatively upon your scholarly ambitions and, hence, they do not expect that you will fail. Since their work will be related in some way to yours, they anticipate that engaging with your work, through reading the thesis, will be an illuminating and uplifting experience. While this may sound strange to you right now, they will also be hoping to learn from your work. The fact that they will be happy to spend a large portion of their time giving thoughtful consideration to your work should be a source of reassurance to you. In return, they expect you will have something important to say and that your findings will shed new light on and advance the field in which they, like you, are immersed.

Very few people are likely to engage with your thesis to the same extent that your examiners do. Even if their viewpoint does not match yours entirely, they will do their best to get 'on the same page' as you. Be aware: they will not necessarily engage with the thesis in the logical progression that you present to them. All readers get a grip of written content in different ways. Take readers of novels, for example. Some like to dip into the beginning and the end before they read the whole novel. They like to sneak a look at the ending before they should. Others scan the chapters quickly before settling down to read through systematically. Still others read methodically from start to finish without any prior scoping. The same is true of the readers of your thesis. If you can't assume that your reader will progress through in the order your chapters are presented, then you will need to be absolutely sure that there is a logical coherence and a strong consistency throughout the thesis. Note what one examiner has written:

*"**Examiner:** First, I must admit to finding the thesis very disorganised. There are so many issues with the general layout and presentation of the thesis that these significantly detract from the work. I consider it essential that these be addressed before the thesis could be considered to be an acceptable standard. It would appear that the candidate has not been given, or not taken, advice on the logical flow of the thesis as a whole. The disorganisation makes it very difficult to follow the thesis and it is not acceptable to expect the reader to put all this together – the thesis needs to tell a logical, linear story, whereas at the moment it is more like a tangled web."*

If you have communicated your ideas clearly and compellingly and created a sense of fascination and wonder through your argument, then, rather than describing it as a 'tangled web', your examiner, as when reading a gripping novel, will find the thesis difficult to put down.

Examiners' reports are usually several pages long, but just as a short report is not an indicator of exemplary work, a long report will not indicate that the thesis is marginal. Some reports will follow the format preferred by the university and some may follow the chapter headings. Some may follow the conventions of the discipline, while others will take their own trajectory. Whatever the format, all reports will make a number of observations that, taken together, will assess the suitability of the thesis for the award of a doctoral qualification. By now you will be quite familiar with what they will be looking for. Briefly, to remind you, the observations they make will be related to:

- the comprehensiveness of the study and its contribution to knowledge
- a familiarity with and understanding of the relevant literature
- the articulation of the research questions
- the identification of research methods and their justification and application
- the honest reporting of the findings
- the careful analysis of the findings and their relevance within the wider context of knowledge
- the quality of English and general presentation.

What the examiners are particularly looking for is your ability to undertake original research. They are also looking for intellectual depth and rigour and a demonstration of your independence as a researcher. Virtually flawless presentation and evidence of your theoretical underpinnings and of a sound methodology as well as a range of skills – creative skills, higher-level thinking skills and analytical skills – will all be searched for. Most of all, the examiners will be looking for the 'X factor' in your work and your point of differentiation from other work. They want to be able to assess the thesis as one that commands respect within the field.

We will spend some time looking at comments from examiners that point to some deficiencies. Examiners will look carefully to see if the research questions have been addressed. They will want to be prepared in the introduction for what follows and they need to know the rationale and assumptions made within the problem definition. They will want to know where you fit into the discussion.

*"**Examiner:** The candidate needs to reflect on her position as researcher within this study. While 'objectivity' is not deemed a virtue within narrative*

inquiry, there needs to be in-depth consideration of how such research was conducted with rigour. How did the candidate monitor biases and subjectivities when it is clear that she entered the fieldwork with strong feelings about previous experiences relevant to the study?"

Examiners will want to know how you define your key terms and concepts. They will be looking for a review of the literature that integrates and synthesises findings from a range of relevant studies. While they do not expect you to synthesise all the available literature sources on your topic, they will expect you to tell them what you believe are the strengths and weaknesses of the most relevant and the seminal studies in the field.

"Examiner: The candidate tends to present and summarise material that she has read rather than synthesising this information and presenting a critical argument to build a coherent conceptual framework for the study. The ensuing discussion appears to lack comprehensive understanding of the key terms used in the study. For example, there is little more than passing attention paid to the central concept of identity and an insufficient differentiation between and coherent discussion of the constructs of beliefs, values, attitudes and confidence which are at the heart of a psychological study on affect."

Examiners will be looking for strong connections between your work and the wider literature. They want to see a clear demonstration of your critical evaluation of the existing body of knowledge in relation to your work. In the evaluation of the literature, they expect to see your work positioned at the centre of the debate and a discussion of the links which will generate new knowledge and which will enhance new thinking.

"Examiner: The thesis is not adequately situated in relation to the literature on childhood obesity. At the very least the literature review needs to explain how the themes being pursued compare and contrast with the literature. Currently the review treads its own path without adequate acknowledgement of earlier attempts to address similar or related themes. Overall, the thesis presents itself as being on the fringe of debate. It would present a more powerful argument if it was located more centrally. Since all readers will not necessarily be sympathetic to the novel arguments put forward, it is important that the candidate supports his arguments as soundly as possible to avoid charges that he is not sufficiently familiar with the field."

The methodology chapter needs to be expressed in a way that would allow any other researcher to replicate the study. Methodological decisions that are made with careful thought make coherent links between the purpose of the research, the information and data needed, the ways in which data are collected and analysed, and the numbers of kinds of participants in the study.

*"**Examiner:** There are some important weaknesses in the research design. The chapter begins by offering a broad unsubstantiated statement that demonstrates discomfort with quantitative approaches and speculates that a 'holistic' and grounded approach might be beneficial. A simple statement of the value of mixed methods would have been more effective than stark demarcation between quantitative and 'holistic' approaches.*

Why didn't the candidate choose fewer case studies and go into more depth with them? How was the volume of data accumulated from case studies managed? What guided the analysis of the data? How exactly was mixed methods used in this study and how was it used for triangulation?

The sampling strategy was developed from an established database but it would have been useful to know how this database was compiled and how comprehensive it is. Some descriptive statistics comparing the sample to the population characteristics would usefully provide an estimate of sample bias.

The questionnaire was sent out as a mail survey. Was there a separate list of topics/questions used in the in-depth interviews? It seems as though additional questions were asked. If so, it would be good to have this list of questions/topics as an appendix as well.

Did the candidate do all the interviews alone? Since interviews lasted between 15 minutes and 3 hours, was there a difference in the candidate's depth of understanding acquired for each of these interviews?"

Examiners will expect to read about the assumptions you have grounded your research in – in relation to the form and nature of the reality being studied and in relation to what constitutes knowledge of the reality being studied. Since different world views generate different theories, from those assumptions the examiners will be able to see the connections between the theory that frames your analytic work, or the theory that you generate.

*"**Examiner:** The main concern about methods relates to the question of using grounded theory and yet failing to develop any theory. As the candidate herself argues, 'A theory of the phenomenon being studied must be developed and explained, and be more than a descriptive account' (p. 53). I remain far from convinced that what has been offered is anything more than a descriptive account."*

Examiners will want to see evidence of critical analysis grounded to the literature, rather than generalisations based on your own beliefs. They will want to see evidence from your research integrated into an argument to support the inferences you make from your interpretations of the data.

*"**Examiner:** In some respects the thesis reads less like a contribution to the literature than like a technical report in which a contemporary phenomenon had been expertly described and analysed. Quite apart from this thesis, if the*

candidate hopes to publish his work in quality academic journals, I think he will be expected to answer the question: 'How does this paper advance theory?'"

You will need to substantiate your claims and set out the significance of your findings in the context of previous research. The examiners will want to see a logical fit between the analytical methods used and the research questions and data collection methods. Some analytical methods, more than others, will have a greater fit within your research design.

*"**Examiner:** I am not convinced by the approach taken to develop those themes and that is the approach of discourse analysis. Arguably, there are many possible interpretations of discourse analysis. However, a Foucauldian approach looks at texts with a specific focus in mind and that is to unpack the relationship between power and knowledge within processes and structures. The instances of text provided are not analysed in any structured way. Rather, they are presented as self-evidential arguments that the researcher wants to make. Given the Foucauldian approach signalled in the paper, there is a need here to draw out the point that the views of the participants are located in sites of knowledge production that are inevitably political."*

Examiners expect to read a logical and coherent argument presented with attention to grammar and free from typographical errors. If there is one thing that is guaranteed to put your examiner off right from the beginning, it is a thesis full of spelling mistakes, grammatical errors and issues in relation to graphs and statistical analysis. Under no circumstances should you submit a half-baked or borderline thesis with the expectation that your examiners will strengthen your weak draft by pointing out the errors of your ways and salvage the thesis for you.

*"**Examiner:** The paper needs a thorough edit with specific attention given to grammar and logical sequence of ideas. Too many sentences are overly long. The use of semi-colons that serve the purpose of adding a new idea into the sentence should be avoided. Some 'sentences' are in fact not sentences and some sentence arguments do not follow logically from the preceding one. Attention to these important details is imperative and would allow the reader to make more sense of the discussion."*

The examiners' remarks might seem overly harsh but they are the kind of remarks that you must do your best to avoid. To be sure, some of the comments above relate to marginal standards, but, even so, you should be aware that students sometimes overestimate the quality of their thesis and, as a result, take a hard knock when examiners provide negative comments. If you have followed the advice in this book, the feedback you will receive will be centred around your examiner's assessment of your thesis as being of sufficient standard (with some possible changes) to merit a doctoral qualification. The feedback often reflects the level of the examiner's engagement with the thesis and is intended to move your work forward even further. Consider the feedback you receive as constructive criticism.

The viva or defence (oral examination)

The viva or defence (oral) is the second component in the examination process. It complements and adds strength to the written reports of the examiners. It is not a mere formality but a significant part of the examination process. The full term 'viva voce' means, literally, 'with the living voice' (indicating that we are talking here about something spoken). It comes from a practice in medieval Europe when scholarly status was granted to individuals who were able to demonstrate their knowledge by responding to questions from the public, and on any subject. The historical link with present-day practices is noticeable in both the United States and in European universities where the tradition of public or semi-public defence of the thesis is still practised. However, current practice is not as nerve-wracking for the student as in earlier times. In current settings, the knowledge focus is only on the thesis and, by the time the defence takes place (sometimes with family and friends as audience), the doctorate will be nearing endorsement from the examining committee. Whether you are based in the United States, in Europe, or anywhere else where the viva or defence takes place, the conferment of scholarly doctoral status is the objective.

Why do universities tend to insist on an oral examination when they already have mechanisms in place to assess the written examination? One reason is that it is a way of ensuring that you are the author of the thesis and you are the person who undertook the research. Authenticity is particularly important if your research involved you working with a team of researchers. It is also important in cases where there is a possibility that you were merely following instructions from the supervisor, performing the role of research assistant rather than researcher. Examiners will want to be satisfied that you have made an original as well as a significant contribution and that you have a clear understanding of all the facets of the research as written in the thesis.

A second reason for requiring a viva or defence is to confirm the quality of the thesis and clarify weak areas. Examiners will expect you to discuss and defend the content and the line of argument that the thesis advances. They will also want you to justify all the decisions made and to acknowledge the limits and boundaries created by those decisions. If the examiners are satisfied that you are able to address all these issues adequately, then you will be recognised as a future member of the research community who commands respect.

The viva or defence process works this way in many universities. Once the examiners' written reports are submitted and shared amongst the examiners, the viva or defence is arranged; often, a convenor or chair is appointed who will meet with you prior to the examination to tell you about the process and, if possible, to show you the room where the viva will be held. Two of your examiners will participate in the examination whilst the third examiner is simply invited to provide questions for discussion. Before the examination the two examiners who are attending will meet to share views on the thesis and to sort out which questions to ask and the order in which they will be asked.

Your supervisor will often be invited to attend the examination but will not be able to participate actively. The supervisor's role is one of support for you during the examination. Once the examination gets underway the chair will welcome everyone, tell you the way the meeting will be structured, and then ask you to speak for around ten minutes about your work. When you have finished your presentation the examiners will ask you their questions. On completion, which should take between one and two hours, you and your supervisor leave the examination whilst the examiners deliberate on their recommendation. When they are agreed, the chair then calls you back to let you know what the recommendation is. At this point, if you have not already received them, you will be given the examiners' reports. Later you will be sent the list of emendations, a date by which the changes are to be completed, and a notification concerning who will sign the thesis off.

Activity

Check out the policies at your university related to the doctoral viva or defence.
  In particular:

1. How many examiners will be in attendance?
2. Are your supervisors expected to attend?
3. Are you expected to present a summary of your research?
4. Will you be able to see the examiners' reports before the viva or defence?
5. What constitutes minor emendations?
6. What constitutes major emendations?

You need to know what the outcomes might be. One *unlikely* outcome is that the examiners recommend you be awarded the doctorate with no further work to do. To be frank, this outcome happens so rarely that it is not worth contemplating. Another *unlikely* outcome is that you will not be recommended for a doctoral award but will be recommended a lesser award or a fail. This outcome is unlikely simply because if you have worked diligently on your project under the watchful eye of your supervisor for around four years, and have your supervisor's blessing for the work, then it is highly probable that you will have fulfilled the necessary criteria for consideration for the award of a doctorate. What is *most likely* to happen is that you will be recommended the award of a doctorate, subject to minor or major emendations. That means that some further work is required. In very occasional situations where the examiners believe that a major rewrite or further research is necessary in order to bring the work up to doctoral standard, the examiners 'refer' the thesis and ask that once the changes are made the thesis is re-examined.

All this sounds very straightforward, and most vivas and defences *are* straightforward (but they are never entirely predictable; examiners are people, after all). Most proceed in a fair and professional fashion. However, occasionally things do not go according to plan. Examiners do take their responsibility seriously and are very keen to carry out their task in a right and proper way. Now and then they push that responsibility to the extreme so that their reading becomes focused on every little error and on producing long lists of minor faults. In the process they fail to engage with the big picture and the central argument presented in the thesis. It does happen that an examiner comes along with tunnel vision, just as it happens that some examiners focus on impressing rather than engaging, or come to the viva with an axe to grind. Things very quickly turn upside down.

Case study

Jim entered the examination room feeling fairly confident. From his longitudinal study on self-protective behaviours within corporate environments he developed a model of predictive behaviours in specific workplace settings. He had found the doctoral experience particularly stimulating and enriching. In the written reports, his overseas examiner (who was not required to attend the viva) passed it, claiming it as 'ground breaking'. The other external examiner assessed it as 'good' and passed it with minor emendations. The internal examiner, however, had a major problem with the methodology. The external examiner who passed it with emendations changed his view in the viva on the basis that he didn't know enough about the internal examiner's argument and decided that because of that, the internal must be correct. Neither of the examiners present put forward the overseas examiner's perspective. Most of the 90 minutes of the viva was taken up with the internal examiner taking a confrontational stance to the thesis.

It is most unlikely that your viva will be the scene of confrontation. Rather, you can expect that your viva will take the form of a stimulating discussion amongst scholars with more than a passing interest in your topic. The rite of passage that many people talk about in relation to the viva or defence is far better represented as a face-to-face discussion about your work with a small group of people who share a commitment to scholarly values. Consider your presence at the viva as a rare and enriching experience in which you can explain your decisions, share the significance of your important findings and demonstrate your capabilities and specialist knowledge. The examiners, meanwhile, will relish the opportunity to hear you explain what you did and the decisions you made. While they have an important task to carry out (verifying your authorship and confirming that your thesis is of a quality which merits a doctorate), in performing that task, naturally, they will have to probe to get an in-depth grip of the work. In asking their questions they will usually do their very best to make you feel at ease. Some are better at this than others.

> **"**I gave my presentation and then it was straight into the questions and no nice warm-up questions or anything, just straight, right, into: 'On page such and such you talk about the differences between qualitative and quantitative methodology and you say that you are using a mixed method methodology. But you don't seem to talk about the quantitative stuff as much as you do about the qualitative stuff. Why is that?' And that was the first question.**"**

Whatever the approach, they are certainly not there to set traps for you with their high-level questions. Their key interest is in hearing about your views on the current status of your topic area and your particular contribution.

● Preparing for the viva or defence

By the time your viva or defence is in sight, a considerable number of weeks – possibly months – will have passed by and you will have moved on to other things. The thesis begins to feel neither fresh nor new. You might begin to wonder how you could have become so engrossed in it for so long. Worse, you might worry that the work is not as far reaching and ground breaking as you thought it would be. These are, you will be pleased to know, the same kinds of concerns that most students have. The secret is to trust in the good judgement of your supervisor.

> **"**I feel quite confident [about the prospect of the viva]. I feel pretty good, if you catch me on a good day. I mean, there are always times when you think, oh, you're not sure. But a lot of the confidence comes from my main supervi-

sor who has a very long and successful track record in successful doctoral students – students who pass their vivas. So when she says this is ready, I trust her. And when she tells me it's good then I trust her judgement on that, because I don't have the experience so the only thing I can do is trust her judgement."

Talking about your work in a way that is convincing to experts in the field is quite different from writing about what you did and found and the significance of the findings. No matter how linguistically elegant your written thesis might be, it is not until the viva that you join the scholarly debate around your topic in person. The way you articulate your thoughts about the work and the way you present yourself at the viva will play a critical role in the assessment of your work. It is unlikely that you will be able to sit in on another student's viva to get a sense of what works well and what does not work so well. However, if you have the opportunity of watching a recording of a viva, either real or simulated, then the advice is, do not hesitate to follow this up. In viewing the presentation, notice all the non-verbal behaviours, such as posture, gestures and facial expressions, along with the tone of voice. Consider what they tell you about the student's involvement in the research.

You may not, understandably, feel at all comfortable with the prospect of speaking about what you did and found and the significance of your findings. The prospect of responding to questions in an intelligent way when the examiners' eyes and minds are focused directly on you is understandably daunting. If thinking on your feet in this context feels like an impossible task, then it is critical that you have the experience of presenting your work before the event. You may have presented at conferences or seminars along the doctoral journey and have learned from those experiences. If not, then consider seriously the notion of presenting a summary of your work to your writing support group or at least to your supervisor. Practise your summary talk and use the feedback your audience gives you to improve. Using a PowerPoint® presentation or other visual or print aid is an ideal way to take the audience's eyes off you and onto a screen or page. But use the aids with a clear purpose in mind and, of course, only when the university makes provision for their use.

Now let us suppose you are well practised and are making final practical arrangements for the viva or defence. Make absolutely sure of the date and time and check out the examination venue ahead of time. Give yourself plenty of time to travel to the venue and, if you live some distance away, make plans to arrive the day before the viva to avoid traffic delays. Decide what you will wear to the examination and, if there is no recommended dress code, prepare appropriately for the formal occasion. Gather together your 'survival' kit containing your thesis, pen, paper, prepared notes, and drinking water. Don't forget to prepare a backup of your PowerPoint, if you plan to present one, and check before the event that the technology provided in the examination room is working.

Case study

Stanley had worked hard on his preparation for the viva. He had practised his presentation with his supervisor and fellow doctoral students and taken advice from his audience. His written thesis included a number of diagrams and tables, which he decided, for ease of discussion, to add into a PowerPoint presentation. At the viva the technology failed and he had to manage without it. However, there were two things that helped him deal with this issue: the first was that he was confident about his work and could explain his research reasonably clearly with or without the technological aid. The second point was that his supervisor came to his assistance by asking for a short delay before the viva commenced, during which time she printed off the slides relating to the diagrams so that Stanley could refer to the detail in them more readily.

● Your role in the viva or defence

Let us imagine, now, that the time has now come and the viva or defence is about to begin. After the introductions, you will be asked to provide your short presentation. Since your thesis is a very long document it would be impossible to speak about everything, so you have sensibly created a synopsis of the sections you feel are important for the examiners to know about or at least to reflect upon. You summarise earlier research in the area, describe your research design and methodology, and the theory that framed your work, and, of course, you talk about your findings. Since you truly want to engage your examiners, you speak to them in a way that is easy for them to follow. In speaking to them you use the past tense since you are talking about events that have already happened. Whether you are putting forward your argument, explaining the decisions you made, providing a background to the study or summarising the findings, you find yourself talking confidently and slowly, for effect, making strategic use of pauses. You use eye contact with your examiners and you try to appear professional and, even if you might not feel it, moderately confident.

You are fully aware that your examiners will be keen for you to clarify what your contribution has been to the discipline. They will want to know in what respect you believe your research has advanced understandings in the field. There are many ways in which doctoral students make a contribution to the field. For example, the topic area might be under-researched in the literature; a different kind of analysis to a pressing problem has been offered; the methodology is novel in the field of study; the theoretical framework used is innovative and has informed the analysis. Your examiners will be expecting you to tell them precisely what *your* point of differentiation is from other work in the area. You will have prepared for this and will have woven a discussion about your research contribution into your presentation. Since you don't want to overemphasise this aspect in your presentation, you plan to elaborate further on it during the questions-and-answers component of the viva.

When you have completed your presentation it will be time for you to respond to the questions that the examiners put to you. Listen carefully and take particular care that you wait until the examiner has completely finished asking the question before you offer your answer. You may want to write the question down to help you grasp it. Or you may want to refer to the copy of your thesis you have brought along. Some of the questions, particularly early on in the questioning, may seem relatively inconsequential to your important work but you will need to show a mark of respect no matter what your thoughts are about the relevance or intellectual depth of each question. 'Small talk' questions, particularly, may be an examiner's strategy to help you feel at ease.

When confronted with a question you do not understand, ask the questioner to repeat it. If the question takes you by surprise, then pause. Let the examiners wait while you gather your thoughts; they don't expect you to have ready answers all the time. Or you might want to consider saying: 'That idea/proposal/connection hadn't occurred to me but my findings would suggest that ...' If you cannot see any link between your work and the question, then let the examiner know that you do not know the answer. Be honest rather than pretend to know. It may surprise you to know that you will not necessarily be expected to know all the answers, so don't be alarmed by a question beyond your expertise and knowledge.

The examiners are seeking to engage you in a collegial discussion, so you must give them the courtesy of joining in that discussion. They may ask why you did this research. They may ask you to explain in a few words the answers your research provided to your research questions. They might ask you about earlier work on the topic and the key researchers involved as well as the strengths and the limitations of the early body of work. They may ask you about your particular research design, and your sample of participants and your data-gathering method. They may ask you to explain the theory that supports your analysis. They may ask you to explain your interpretations. In fact, they may ask any number of questions that you feel should be self-explanatory from your thesis. Take heart: these questions are not meant to imply that there are problems with the literature review, with the methodology, with the theory or with the analysis. The questions are simply to put the examiners' minds at ease with regard to your knowledge and your reasons for carrying out the research in the way it was carried out. They want to be sure that *you* (and not your supervisor or anyone else) know exactly what was done and that you can justify the decisions made.

Since the examiners are very keen to validate your work, be sure that you are able to provide clear explanations. This means that you will need to be fully familiar with everything in your thesis, including statistical display and analysis of data. In that respect, if there are any statistical aspects unclear to you, it would be advisable to seek assistance from knowledgeable statistical analysts before the examination. Be sure, too, that you are able to provide justifications for the numerous decisions made in relation to the research. The viva is definitely not the place to argue against what you have done or to draw attention to any errors in the thesis. Rather, it is a place where you convince the examiners of your confidence in the work you have undertaken. They want to be sure that your work marks you out as a competent researcher.

Of course, there are likely to be questions from the examiners that seem to stretch you to the limit. Stay calm and, at all costs, do not become aggressive or defensive. Don't forget that you will know a lot more about your topic than your examiners. Since your examiners are keen to learn about a topic that has consumed your interest over the past few years, they may need to ask a number of sharp questions to clarify doubts or ambiguities. Often, the way they do that is to advance a proposition that will challenge your position. For example, they might say something like, 'You could have addressed your research questions using action research design rather than ethnography. What makes ethnography so special in your research?' Or, 'Brown's interpretations are quite at odds with yours. Can you explain that fact?' In asking these kinds of questions, the examiners are interested to see if you can rise to the challenge and defend your work.

And of course you *can* rise to their challenge. If you practised before the viva with your writing group, you will be aware of other ways of thinking about your work and the need to prepare responses to challenges. Since you know more than anybody else about your specific area of investigation, you will respond to contradictory proposals from the examiners as though you were participating in a debate. Like a good debater, you will not necessarily agree with the examiner's proposition. Like a good debater, you will offer a rebuttal by defining your position (even if this means repeating information you have already provided) and then defending it, highlighting how your specific position adds more strength to your overall argument than the contradictory position proposed.

There may be a discussion about your publication plans; then, before you know it, the examiners' questions – and, with them, the collegial discussion – will draw to an end. This is the time to politely thank the examiners for their close and insightful reading of your thesis. The chair will then ask you and your supervisors to leave the room in order for the examiners to discuss your suitability for the award and to make their final recommendation. At this time they will agree on what emendations will be required (if any) and the time frame for those emendations. Then you will be invited back into the room with your supervisor. The examiners' anonymous reports and their recommendation, including the list of emendations and the name of the person who will be responsible for confirming the changes, will be given to you.

Since your examiners are likely to remain in the room while this information is presented to you, accept the recommendation graciously. You might like to express your gratitude to the examiners for the valuable experience and for their careful consideration of how the work could be strengthened. Given what you know about viva outcomes, you should be well prepared to make some concessions to your work for your examiners. Typically, everyone who has been present at the viva is comfortable with the outcome. In very unusual cases, a student may have grounds to appeal the decision. Each university has its own procedures for appeal. The appeal may possibly be made on the grounds of inappropriate standards used for the assessment of the research, or because of supervision inadequacy, or possibly because of the student's extreme personal extenuating circumstances.

Since you are unlikely to be appealing the decision, you and your supervisor can breathe a sigh of relief and celebrate the fact that you put your best foot forward in the viva. The decision will likely mean further work, and since you will want to get the thesis signed off as soon as possible, the best approach is to tackle the emendations, with the support of your supervisor, as soon as possible. Once you have dealt with the revisions to the satisfaction of your supervisor (or other person assigned to the task), you can send the thesis on its way for final binding. The next phase is sign-off by the Council – and then your graduation. You have finally conquered it. Congratulations, doctor!

In the next and final chapter we shift our focus to the stage when the thesis examination is over and any emendations have been approved. We explore the avenues for getting your research 'out there' into the research and wider communities. We look at the requirements for writing for academic publications and to writing for professional journals. Publications as well as presentations and media reports are all valuable means available for disseminating your work. They all represent ways to demonstrate the beginning of your life as a professional researcher.

Review

Main points:
- There are typically two parts to the examination process: examination of the written thesis and a viva or defence.
- There are likely to be three examiners.
- The nomination of names of examiners needs to be considered carefully.
- Examiners anticipate that they will learn more about your topic as a result of reading your thesis.
- Examiners each provide an independent written report on your work.
- The viva is an examination of your verbal account of the research and is designed to confirm your authenticity and to confirm the quality of the thesis.
- Two examiners and often your supervisor and a chair will attend your viva.
- Typically you will present a short summary of your research and will answer questions put to you by the examiners.
- The examiners expect you to engage in scholarly discussion with them about your work and at the end of the viva will provide a recommendation of the award.
- Appeals may be lodged in rare cases.
- When you have completed any emendations required, the thesis is bound in its final form and your work is then approved by the official governing body.

Key terms:
- Written thesis examination
- The viva or defence
- Emendations

9 Getting Your Research 'Out There'

This chapter looks at:

- ▶ Beyond the thesis
- ▶ Publishing journal articles
- ▶ Submission and reviewing processes
- ▶ Books
- ▶ Presentations
- ▶ Future orientation

● Beyond the thesis

Congratulations on getting to this stage! You have completed your emendations and earned the title of doctor. There is no denying, being awarded the degree feels very personally satisfying. Reaching the destination after a long and sometimes arduous journey, you deserve all the accolades you receive. After all, it has taken a consistent effort and sheer determination on your part to get to this point. Now, at the end of the doctoral journey, you know so much more about your chosen topic, and your understanding of intellectual argument and rigour has grown. You know so much more about yourself, too. You have grown both personally and intellectually and probably find it difficult to identify with the person you were when you first began the journey. A new and exciting future is on offer as your life as a doctor stretches before you.

In the euphoria of the moment, spare a few thoughts for those who have supported you on your journey. Take some time to re-engage with family members, to rekindle friendships, and to enjoy the activities that were not possible during your doctoral journey. Take a well-earned holiday. All your hard work and commitment have possibly taken a toll on your well-being and emotions. Many students experience mixed emotions at the completion of a doctorate, such as a sense of being at a loose end, a huge sense of relief, and a lack of motivation. Don't be surprised at these feelings but try not to let them take charge. Move on to a new project – and, quite frankly, there is no better project than to share your newfound knowledge with others.

Interestingly, very few doctoral theses are read by anyone other than the supervisors and examiners. You simply can't count on your thesis as the defining document that will establish your mark as a scholar. After all the time and effort you have given to your topic area it does not make a lot of sense to let your thesis contribution gather dust on a library shelf. It makes even less sense if you are hoping to become a professional researcher. If you want to make a contribution to the scholarly conversation around your topic you will have to get your work 'out there'. Others will want to be made aware of your new ideas, your innovative analyses and your findings. Let them know how your new knowledge challenges the literature and, in that capacity, how it advances the discipline and empowers the profession. Don't hesitate in getting your work out there; the longer you leave your entrée into the disciplinary conversation, the more difficult it will be to make a contribution. Hard as it might be to swallow, you need to recognise that your leading-edge work will soon become outdated.

If you want to join the community of professional researchers, a guaranteed route is through publications. An academic trajectory is determined by what you publish. The chief means of advancing your academic career will be through publications in peer-reviewed journals or in books with reputable publishers, just as your academic career will be severely curtailed by a lack of publications. The hard fact is that universities look more favourably upon an application for an academic appointment when the application is accompanied by evidence of capability to publish. A publication portfolio, necessarily small at this stage, will hold you in good stead.

If your aspiration is not with the academy then it is likely that your new knowledge will benefit the professional community, the policy arena or the commercial field. You will still seek publication in academic journals to share your new knowledge with your fellow researchers, since your doctorate will be publishable, in part at least. However, you might be more attracted to reporting your work in non-refereed publications of professional associations and in conference proceedings. You might also be highly interested in reporting on your work through newspapers, magazines and Internet blogs, as well as by speaking about your work on television and radio in order to gain a wider social outreach and generate interest in your specific topic area. Presentations to practitioners and policy makers might also hold appeal.

Whatever your professional destination, you need others to read and hear what you have to say. Getting your work 'out there' to a wider audience is the primary means by which you are able to have an influence on the thinking within your discipline. However, getting your work 'out there' involves planning. It requires you to establish a personal programme of writing, and regular protected writing time, to accomplish your publication plans. Consider the different aspects of your thesis and work out how each of those aspects that you want to share with others could be constructed to offer new knowledge. Quite likely you will be able to see how, from different kinds of papers, the discipline, the profession and policy makers could all benefit from your new knowledge. Figure out the order in which you will write these separate papers.

Getting your work 'out there' will require you to think creatively in order to find a space in the current academic, professional and policy conversations where you can make a contribution. Being flexible and making connections will allow you to add to the current conversation. Bear in mind that no one in the research community wants the current conversation completely stifled by a newcomer, so your particular 'take' has to be both compatible with and respectful of the investment that the research community has already made in the conversation. What the community will be particularly interested in is reading and hearing the issues and questions that concern them most addressed in new ways.

● Publishing journal articles

Breaking into the journal publishing scene may not be as intimidating as you think. Your supervisors will want you to publish your work and may even collaborate with you. They want you to get published because in that way others will get to know about and value the kind of work you do. Your examiners may also have noted potential publications suitable for your work. Publishing your work opens up lasting opportunities. The fascinating thing about getting published is that your publication will never die. It will go on forever. You might not have thought about it in those terms before.

Journal editors, too, will want to publish your exciting ideas and new approaches. They are very keen to support early career researchers who are scholarly writers. They are particularly interested in research that explores new questions or investigates existing issues and problems in a fresh way. They like to read about carefully interpreted data that question earlier findings. They are intrigued by creative research designs, innovative or simplified theoretical frameworks, and searching analyses. They are also on the lookout for articles that have major implications at the level of practice. Since at least one of these situations will apply to your doctoral thesis, they will want to read your work.

There will be obvious areas within your thesis that will be suitable for publication. For example, if your research was focused around three case studies, then each of these cases might be developed into an article. There are many other examples. You might choose to write a theoretical article in order to showcase a new framework and to demonstrate its relevance to the discipline. You might have written a particularly strong literature review that could be reworked for a journal. A pilot study or other work that did not find its way into the thesis might also provide suitable material for a journal article.

Activity

Publication plan: Write as many entries as you can to complete the table.

Theme of publication	Targeted journal or conference proceedings	Deadline for completed	Chapter(s) in thesis to draw upon	Word limit and any special requirements for publication

However, you may not initially be interested in writing a full journal article. There are other options. For example, you might consider writing for a journal that accepts shorter articles. You might be interested in writing research notes, or a commentary, or for another category, such as 'research around the world', that the journal makes available. Each of these categories, if made possible within the journal, will have predetermined word limits with which you must comply. The thing is that you must think about and plan your publications strategically. There is no magic to publishing – just things to learn and things to plan.

In preparing your work for journal submission, the first point to note is that there is a hierarchy of journals. During the course of your doctorate you may well have become aware of which journals are the highest ranking in your discipline, and, if that is the case, you will probably have noted the journal's impact score. In simple terms, the impact score (impact factor, IF) is a measure of citation. Specifically, a high impact score of just over or around 1 means that every paper published in the high-ranking journal is cited one or more times within five years by another paper in a range of given journals. A glance at the distinguished names listed on the editorial board will also be an indicator of the high standing of the journal. Papers in high-ranking journals do tend to carry more status.

Whilst publishing in a highly prestigious journal with a wide circulation is bound to accelerate your academic opportunities, it may not be your immediate goal. In that case, you might consider publishing in a journal with an impact score of around 0.5. You might also want to consider publishing in a more focused and specialist journal, in a journal published only online, in a localised journal, or in a professional journal. A major consideration for you if English is not your first language is whether to publish in English or in your home language. You need to be aware that your work will reach a wider audience if you publish in English. Aspiring authors of English journal publications soon come to appreciate differences in focus, if not from their own reading, then from the editorial statements of intent published within the journal. You will also come to an understanding of the standard, readership and circulation.

The second point, given your knowledge of the differences between journals, is to target your journal. It is much easier to get published if your article is compatible with the journal's mission and focus and with the interests of its readers. Will it be appropriate to write about a single case study and analyse qualitative data? Your article on teaching practices in a remote school in the Australian outback, for example, is probably not going to make it in a journal that promotes quantitative methodologies to determine learners' achievement outcomes. Will your theoretical framing be deemed too radical or inappropriate for the journal's readers? As an example, a highly theoretical article on systems analysis is not likely to get past the first post in a workplace practitioners' journal. Select a journal where the match between yours and the journal's focus is closely aligned.

The third point is that once you have targeted your journal, you need to target your audience. Your journal article writing will not be the same as the writing you presented in your thesis, so it is highly unlikely that you will be able to transport entire sections from your thesis into the article. In the thesis the reader was your examiner. You took great pains to guide the examiner through each step of the way and to map out your argument slowly and carefully. In contrast, the reader of your journal article is an academic peer who is not interested in examining the fine detail of your work. He or she wants to learn something new about the field and will not be interested in every last detail concerning your reasons for undertaking the research and your methodological decisions. Nor will the reader be interested in your comprehensive literature review and in learning about your full findings. Since the examiner and the article reader will engage with your work differently, your journal article writing will need to meet your reader's purpose.

In many ways, writing a journal article means conforming to a genre quite different from your thesis. Your doctoral thesis might have ticked all the right boxes for examiners who are experts in the field but may not be written for a more general peer audience. You need to be clear and focused if you hope to capture the reader's attention. Let us look first at the content. Allowing for differences in style amongst journals, in many cases you will need to provide an abstract, an introduction, a review of the literature and theoretical framing, a methods section, findings and discussion, and a list of references. Have you been able to capture the reader's attention through the content under the various headings? Look at the abstract and make sure your keywords are there. Now look at the first section. Does it capture interest? Look further and ask if the reader knows enough about the context and what you did for them to engage with your paper. How much detail can be assumed and, hence, how much 'padding' can be deleted?

Make it easier for your reader to engage with your work by writing it as a stand-alone piece. The focus of the work should be sufficiently narrow yet pitched at a level sufficiently deep for the reader to grasp your unique contribution. Do your homework and examine recent copies of articles published by the journal in order to determine what issues are being discussed and how you might enter into the discussion and debate. Emphasise early on what you bring new to the academic conversation and the ways in which your work connects with what has already been said. Explain how your frameworks, methodology or findings address, in new ways, the questions and issues that are important to the journal's focus.

Style and presentation are all-important. Avoid jargon and complex sentences. Instead, use simple sentence-level grammar to develop a sense of cohesion through the themes you construct in your paper. Does your paper conform to the structure and writing conventions of the journal? Check the organisation of published papers in the journal so that you are sure. While you are doing that, check that your citations and references conform to the journal's style guidelines. Clarify your definitions and take extreme care over any claims made in your analysis. Report honestly about the way things turned out and do not overlook the importance of careful revision and editing of your work.

Below is an example of the guidelines that might be available to prospective authors of any journal on its website. Journals do not operate as secret societies. They are transparent in their methods.

Example of criteria for journal authors

1. The paper should make a significant contribution to the furtherance of knowledge.
2. Manuscripts should not have appeared in other journals.
3. Articles must be relevant to the focus of the journal.
4. The journal is willing to publish papers following any research paradigm.
5. Papers may be of any length up to 7000–8000 words.
6. The paper should read well. It should have a good flow, and be logically organised.
7. The paper should be clearly written in good English.
8. Use APA 6th edition for a guide to style.

● Submission and reviewing processes

Now we move to the stage when your article is written (generally speaking, we talk of your 'manuscript' rather than your 'article' at this stage). You will need to check the journal's submission guidelines. Typically, you will be required to submit your manuscript through the journal's online submission system. Alternatively, you may be required to email your manuscript directly to the editor. The guidelines will inform you of the number of copies to be sent, and this will usually consist of your full manuscript with your name and details and affiliation, as well as a blind copy of your manuscript with all identifying information deleted, including your name in the citations and references. When submitting your manuscript you should provide a covering note (or an email, if appropriate) requesting that the manuscript be considered for publication in the journal. You should also declare that the manuscript has not previously been published, that it is not under consideration for publication anywhere else, and that all co-authors (if any) have given their approval for the manuscript to be submitted. Not long after you send the manuscript on its way, you will receive notification that it has been received by the journal, that it is deemed suitable for the journal, and that it will be sent out for review.

The first step in your new publishing career is over and your first manuscript will shortly find its way into the hands of experts. You will, of course, have placed an electronic copy of the submitted article in your own safekeeping. While you are waiting for news of its status, you should start working on your second manuscript or your conference presentation or any other writing that will be a vehicle for disseminating your work. Some writers prefer to multi-task and work on more than one article simultaneously, but most of us prefer to focus on one thing at a time. While you are promoting your work through your writing you are likely to receive news of how the manuscript you submitted is progressing. This could be months, even a year or so, from the time you submitted it.

During the long interval, the blind copy of your manuscript (the copy with all identifying information removed) will have been sent to two, three or four experts – including, usually, one editorial board member – who will review your manuscript. Most quality journals operate a double-blind review process, which means that the referee is not provided with the name of the author, and you, likewise, are not provided the name of the reviewer, when you finally receive feedback. In the fullness of time each of the experts (also known as peers and referees) will send in an individual independent report that sets out the expert's views of the manuscript and provides a recommendation concerning publication. Journals tend to depend on the peer review process as the chief quality assurance system for maintaining standards within the journal.

Let us take a little time to explore what referees are looking for in your manuscript. We will do this by identifying ten key rules for authors.

Reviewers' comments listed as ten key rules for authors

1. Thou shalt not have an unclear focus.
2. Thou shalt offer clarity over definitions.
3. Thou shalt be careful with literature reviews.

4. Thou shalt not omit theoretical underpinnings.
5. Thou shalt take care over local/narrow perspectives.
6. Thou shalt not lack methodological transparency.
7. Thou shalt pay due attention to data analysis.
8. Thou shalt not make unjustified claims.
9. Thou shalt not make errors in format or presentation.
10. Thou shalt not report overly positively.

Reviewers tend to be fairly decisive people, particularly when they are providing an anonymous review. We will explore each of their points in turn.

1. **Thou shalt not have an unclear focus.** An unclear focus within a manuscript is an issue reviewers come across all the time. They find themselves asking, 'What exactly was this paper about?' Often they don't know until they get to the end of the paper. On the other hand, authors who confront the 'what?', 'why?', 'what next?', 'so what?' questions make it clear to the reviewer what the focus is all about. They make the research questions explicit and ensure that they report and analyse data that address those questions.
2. **Thou shalt offer clarity over definitions.** Authors often make assumptions that readers understand terms and expressions in exactly the same way as they (authors) do. What's more, authors sometimes use a number of different terms to mean the same thing. Reviewers expect authors to provide clarity over and consistency with terms and expressions used.
3. **Thou shalt be careful with literature reviews.** Journal reviewers raise concerns over reviews that are outdated, insufficient or not linked to the subsequent study reported on. Authors often fail to critically interrogate the literature. As reviewers point out, whether or not authors agree with everything experts have said, the literature that has made a mark on the field should be cited.
4. **Thou shalt not omit theoretical underpinnings.** Reviewers are tending more and more to demand attention to theory. They note that authors fail to provide, articulate, or make transparent, their theoretical perspectives. The framework should be explanatory and should guide the collection and analysis of data. There is also a concern that authors sometimes simply impose a theoretical framework on the data; some simply offer a diagram with arrow links.
5. **Thou shalt take care over local/narrow perspectives.** Reviewers are not saying that your study should not be local. Rather,

what they are saying is that you need to tell them about your particular local context. Do not assume that readers already know about the context.

6. **Thou shalt not lack methodological transparency.** The major criticism here is centred on the research design and methods. There may be inadequate information, or there may be no reasons provided for the choices made about methodology. There may be a flawed sample. Reviewers and readers expect to find sufficient information about the participants, settings, research design, and the methods and approach taken. When the methodology is criticised, most reviewers note that the research approach was inappropriate to address the research question, or that there was a mismatch between the research question and methods used.

7. **Thou shalt pay due attention to data analysis.** Journal reviewers occasionally receive empirical papers that contain no data analysis. They also receive papers in which the data analysis is unsystematic or superficial, and papers in which the data analysis is overly descriptive. Reviewers do not like data tables and charts that are confusing. They also do not like large chunks of qualitative data that do not make a lot of sense.

8. **Thou shalt not make unjustified claims.** Reviewers feel very uneasy about manuscripts that advance claims *on slim evidence*, that advance claims *in spite of evidence*, and manuscripts that have claims *imposed on evidence*. They are also concerned about unsupported generalisations and over-interpretation of evidence. Some reviewers criticise implications and recommendations, as set out by the author, that are not related to or derived from the research findings.

9. **Thou shalt not make errors in format or presentation.** The kinds of things that reviewers note are related to lack of proofreading; a title that is not sufficiently related to, or is totally unrelated to, the text; inconsistencies between abstract and manuscript; lack of internal consistency and lack of coherence between sections; poor grammar; overly long sentences; lack of compliance with word length; undefined abbreviations and acronyms; inadequate punctuation; missing or unused references.

10. **Thou shalt not report overly positively.** In an ideal research world things would turn out just as researchers want them to. But they often do not turn out that way. Reviewers expect authors to be honest in their reporting. They do not want authors to paint a picture of roses. Rather, they want readers to explain the setbacks, the trials, and the things that went wrong.

These are the kinds of issues that reviewers will pay attention to in reviewing your manuscript. When your reviewers have completed their assessment of your manuscript they will send their report to the journal's editor. When all the reviews of your manuscript are received by the journal, the editor will make a decision based on the referees' recommendations as well as the editor's own reading of the manuscript.

Be prepared for the fact that the decision on your manuscript is not likely to be 'accept with no changes'. This happy event occurs very rarely, even to the most experienced of researchers. More likely, the decision will be that minor or major changes are required to bring the manuscript up to publication standard. Sometimes the editor will suggest a resubmission with a new panel of reviewers; sometimes the editor will make the decision to reject the manuscript. In the letter to you the editor will provide some grounds for the decision and will include copies of all the referees' reports received on your manuscript, and, where changes are required, will provide you with guidance for strengthening the article and with a deadline for the revised version of your manuscript.

If you are asked to make major or minor changes or to provide a resubmission, then the advice is to start on the revisions as soon as possible. Of course, you may feel disappointed or even indignant that the editor has not backed your insightful and groundbreaking manuscript in the way you feel he or she should have. You might also think that the decision involves much more work than you wish to devote to the manuscript, and without any guarantee that it will be published. However, you should know that resubmissions have more success than first submissions. You will gain from the effort in the long run.

Occasionally, reviewers provide contradictory standpoints on the same manuscript. If that happens to yours, the editor will steer you in a direction that will seek to resolve the issue. If you want to get published then you need to be clear that it is the editor's word that will ultimately count. Be aware that you do not have to make all the changes requested but you will have to provide a sound reason, written politely, as to why you challenge a particular reviewer's viewpoint. When you resubmit your revised manuscript, provide a covering letter to the editor that outlines the ways in which you have addressed (or the reasons why you have not addressed) the concerns raised in the decision letter and/or in the reviewers' feedback. Be sure to send your revised submission before the due date.

Once you have submitted the revised manuscript after making the substantive or small changes required (as the case may be), the editor may, depending on the extent of the changes requested, decide to send the revision back to the original reviewers for their feedback or, alternatively, may make the decision alone. You may well be required to make further changes, with respect to those originally requested. Further delays are to be expected while this editorial process is worked through. Finally, the message comes through that your paper has been accepted for publication. This news is certainly great cause for celebration! In time, typeset proofs of your manuscript will be sent to you, and not long after you have checked them and given your approval and have entered into a contractual arrangement with the publishers, your article will be published. In reputable journals, the paper will generally appear as an 'online first' article fairly quickly, which means that it becomes accessible on the journal's website. Later, when your article reaches the top of the accepted papers queue, it will be published in the journal. Your article is recognition in itself that you have truly made it within the academic community!

You are entitled to republish your published journal article in a book, either as a chapter in an edited volume or as a piece in a monograph. However, you need to gain the permission of the publisher of the journal to do this and you need to acknowledge the original publication source of the material. The approval process is straightforward and instructions are often set out on the journal's website. While republishing your article in a book is permitted, you would be in breach of the journal's copyright if you sent your accepted or published article to another journal. However, you are allowed to submit any rejected manuscript for consideration to another journal. You may want to make a few changes to the manuscript first, of course, taking on board the feedback from your reviewers. However, virtually every researcher knows how painful rejection can be, simply because virtually every researcher has had a manuscript rejected. This news may surprise you. Experienced researchers will be able to empathise with you, knowing how self-esteem and confidence take a huge drop after rejection.

What you need to know is that rejection of your work does not equate to its being unpublishable. You can get your work published. Experienced researchers tend to wait a few days after receiving the rejection letter, waiting until the dust settles and they can come to terms with the seemingly misguided feedback. Their advice would be to read the reviews again and figure out – with assistance, if necessary, from your supervisor or another experienced researcher – what you might do to get the manuscript back on track, based on the feedback provided. It will be important, first, to determine to which alternative journal the manuscript might be sent and how you might tailor it to the journal's unique focus. Remember: you won't learn from what you do right; you learn from what you do wrong.

● Books

Some doctoral graduates have aspirations to become published book authors by converting their thesis into a research monograph. Many believe, incorrectly, that the task will be a simple matter of a few small changes here and there within the thesis. Unfortunately, the work involved is, invariably, more than anticipated and will likely involve the reworking of much of what you were passionately attached to in your thesis. What is more, the recognition you will receive for a monograph may well be less than that received for a paper in a quality journal. The advice, then, is to look carefully at what is involved before you make the decision to reshape your thesis into a book.

First of all, there is the issue of audience. Like the reader of the journal article, the reader of your monograph is not your examiner. Your reader will be looking for writing that sustains interest throughout the long reading. Essentially, the writing that you undertake for your book is writing undertaken to sell your product. Style and presentation are all-important to selling your product. Length is also critical. Your book needs to be clear and focused and shorter in length if you hope to capture and sustain the reader's attention.

Then there is the issue of a publisher. Publishers offer book contracts to prospective authors with a view to financial gain for the company. Your reworked thesis needs to be marketable. While you, personally, will be deeply fascinated by the topic of your thesis (having invested so much time and effort in the task), you need to ask yourself the difficult question concerning the likelihood that others will be equally intrigued. How likely, then, is it that a publishing company will be interested in your work and in your ideas? We are not talking here of publishers who demand payment from authors in return for publication. Rather, we are talking of reputable publishers who might be able to advance your publishing career. In the final analysis, few commercial publishers will be able to give serious consideration to your proposed monograph.

Books, however, do have a potential of reaching a broader community. They are cited more frequently than journal articles and, because of that, academics and students will get to know your name much more quickly. If you do want to pursue your dream of writing a monograph then you might want to consider a small university press; in that regard, your supervisor may be able to make a recommendation. Or you could make an appointment with a visiting staff member from a reputable publishing company, when he or she is doing the rounds at your university.

If you are fortunate enough in securing interest from a publisher in the contribution that you can make to knowledge in the field, then you will need to prepare a book proposal. Many publishers provide guidelines and headings for the structure of your proposal and most will require the following: a title; a description of the scope of the book; a rationale for the book; a description of the content and a synopsis of each chapter; details concerning the length of the book and any specific additional information relating to the content; the target market; a list of competing volumes; delivery date of manuscript; the author's details and curriculum vitae; and a sample chapter. Before you complete the proposal, it is worth considering contacting a favourable examiner or another well-known researcher to see if they might be interested in writing a foreword for your book. Their involvement may attract a publisher and may provide a greater outreach when the book is published.

When the publisher offers you a contract, and when you have given your agreement to the terms and conditions, you are on your way to becoming a book author.

● Presentations

Presentations to the academic, professional, practitioner and policy communities, to industry and commercial representatives, and to the general public through the media, are all certain ways of getting your work 'out there'. Apart from conferences that will accept your papers based on peer review, all other presentations and the reporting of your work through newspapers, magazines, Internet blogs, television and radio will give you greater freedom and wider outreach to generate interest in your specific topic area.

In your strategic publishing plan you will have identified a number of possible academic conferences that you would like to attend. Obviously, given the conference registration and travel costs, you will need to be selective and identify the conference or conferences that most closely align with your research interests. If you have not yet completed your thesis, you might want to use the conference as a test bed for your ideas. You will be looking for feedback from the audience. On the other hand, if the thesis is 'done and dusted', you might want to share your findings, or you might be interested in trialling a few new ideas before you submit them to a journal.

The great thing about conference attendance is that not only do you get to share your ideas, your findings and your new knowledge face to face with scholars who have common points of interest with your research, you also get the opportunity of forming long-term networks, associations and potential collaborations. Seize the opportunity, because as a newcomer to the academic conference scene, building networks and friendships will be hugely influential in the development of your career.

You will need to plan ahead simply because abstracts or proposals from presenters are required long before the academic conference date. Study the conference website for information about timelines and requirements. Pay particular attention to the time allocated for the presentation and the technology provided to assist in your PowerPoint presentation. Find out whether or not a paper, in addition to the abstract, is required to be submitted, and if so, when and whether the paper will be peer reviewed. While the headings for the paper will be much the same as those required for a journal article, you will find that it is considerably easier to get acceptance for a paper published in conference proceedings than it is for a paper in a journal.

The presentation itself is designed for audience engagement. Speak confidently and slowly, especially if your conference includes international attendees for whom English is not their first language. Offer the background details if you consider them important for understanding what you did and what you found. Remember, you want the audience to engage with your presentation, so do not take them through unnecessary material. Your presentation should note a few key points, and the best presentations always offer a 'take home' message. As with your viva, anticipate and prepare for questions from the audience and use any issues raised during the discussion following your presentation to strengthen your unfinished thesis or your journal article.

There are likely to be other presentations that you want to make to specific groups within the profession and within the community. While you won't need to provide a paper for those presentations, the same principles apply to the actual presentation. Essentially, you want to engage your audience so that you can share your knowledge and so that you can generate discussion. The media might hold attraction for you as a means of communicating your work. However, fronting up to the media successfully is, more often than not, a learned skill. Seek assistance about how you can create a story about your work in a way that captures the interest of the listener or the viewer.

Some academic conferences include poster sessions. These sessions are also a useful forum for getting your work 'out there'. In many ways, the sessions are less daunting. You don't have to confront an audience who may want to debate your ideas vigorously. You are spared the task of a formal presentation and you get the opportunity to talk with like-minded individuals and small groups. Essentially, you are given a time slot to showcase your poster of a predetermined size and/or a display on your laptop. The poster you have prepared will be attractively designed with the main features of and key findings from your study, which you will be able to explain in more detail if required.

● Future orientation

We have arrived at the final section of the book. By now you will be fully aware that doctoral study is not only a privilege but also a complex activity involving processes and procedures that are often unclear. If you have followed the advice offered in the book, you should now have a clear understanding of the skills, the knowledge and the actions necessary for success. The point in doing this has been for you to benefit from an enriching doctoral experience that contributes to the completion of your study in a timely fashion.

Now that you have achieved success in your doctoral study, you will recognise the ways in which your skills base has been enhanced. You have got to this point through dedication, persistence and determination. Your success involved the avoidance of needless mistakes, distractions, risks and dangers. But perhaps more importantly, you succeeded by learning how to maximise the learning opportunities that presented themselves through day-to-day processes and interactions. By taking control of, and responsibility for, your study, you have successfully navigated your way through the experience of a lifetime. This is no mere simple achievement. You are now a fully fledged researcher with important skills and knowledge that will inform, influence and benefit whatever you choose to undertake in the future. Congratulations!

Review

Main points:
- You cannot depend on your thesis as a means for establishing your mark as a scholar.
- Your work needs to be disseminated before it becomes outdated.
- A guaranteed route to advancing your career is through publications.
- Establish a personal programme to accomplish your publication plans.
- A doctoral thesis contains a number of possible beginning points for your publications.
- While publishing in a high-ranking journal will guarantee kudos, publishing in a lower ranked journal will be easier and will still bring recognition.

- Writing in a journal needs to conform to a different style from your thesis.
- The journal's style and submission guidelines are generally posted on the journal's website.
- Reputable journals operate a peer review process.
- Reviewers write independent reports on the manuscript and the editor draws on these and his or her own reading to make a decision on the manuscript.
- A monograph or book written from the thesis will need to rework the material in the thesis.
- Book proposals are submitted to the publishing company for consideration.
- Presentations to a range of different communities enable you to disseminate your findings.

Key terms:
- Journal hierarchy
- Research interest and journal focus compatibility
- Journal submission
- Manuscript
- Double-blind reviewing
- Monograph
- Poster presentation

Further Reading

Benn, K. and Benn, C. (2006). *Professional Thesis Presentation: A Step-by-Step Guide to Preparing Your Thesis in Microsoft Word*. Auckland: Pearson Prentice Hall.

Bryman, A. (2008). *Social Research Methods* (3rd edn). Oxford: Oxford University Press.

Davidson, C. and Tolich, M. (eds) (2007). *Social Science Research in New Zealand: Many Paths to Understanding*. Auckland: Pearson Prentice Hall.

Denscombe, M. 2003). *The Good Research Guide for Small-Scale Social Research Projects* (2nd edn). Maidenhead: Open University Press.

Farkas, D. (2008). *The Smart Way to Your Ph.D.: 200 Secrets from 100 Graduates*. Arlington, MA: Your Ph.D. Consulting.

Finn, J. A. (2005). *Getting a PhD: An Action Plan to Help Manage Your Research, Your Supervisor and Your Project*. New York: Routledge Study Guides.

Pears, R. and Shields, G. (2008). *Cite Them Right: The Essential Referencing Guide* (8th edn). Basingstoke: Palgrave Macmillan.

Punch, K. L. (2005). *Developing Effective Research Proposals* (2nd edn). London: Sage.

Punch, K. L. (2005). *Introduction to Social Research: Quantitative and Qualitative Approaches* (2nd edn). London: Sage.

Walter, M. (2006). *Social Research Methods: An Australian Perspective*. Melbourne: Oxford University Press.

Bibliography

Bourdieu, P. (1990). *In Other Words: Essays Toward a Reflexive Sociology*. Trans. M. Adamson. Cambridge: Polity Press.

Engeström, Y. (1999). Innovative learning in work teams: Analysing cycles of knowledge creation in practice. In Y. Engeström, R. Miettinen and R.-L. Punamäki (eds), *Perspectives on Activity Theory* (pp. 377–404). Cambridge: Cambridge University Press.

Foucault, M. (1977). *Discipline and Punish: The Birth of the Prison*. Trans. A. Sheridan. Harmondsworth: Penguin.

Gadamer, H. G. (1975). *Truth and Method*. London: Sheed and Ward.

Gilling, M. (ed.) (2000). *Research: The Art of Juggling*. Wellington: Massey University.

Lacan, J. (1977). *The Four Fundamental Concepts of Psycho-analysis*. London: Hogarth Press.

Pears, R. and Shields, G. (2008). *Cite Them Right: The Essential Referencing Guide* (8th edn). Basingstoke: Palgrave Macmillan.

Vygotsky, L. (1978). *Mind and Society*. Cambridge, MA: Harvard University Press.

Žižek, S. (ed.) (1998). *Cogito and the Unconscious*. Durham, NC: Duke University Press.

Index